The Cities of Egypt

BY

REGINALD STUART POOLE

KEEPER OF COINS IN THE BRITISH MUSEUM
CORRESPONDENT OF THE INSTITUTE OF FRANCE

اثارهم فى الارض تخبرنا بهم
والكتب فى سير تقص صحاح

The Lay of the Himyerites

ISBN: 978-1-63923-932-0

All Rights reserved. No part of this book maybe reproduced without written permission from the publishers, except by a reviewer who may quote brief passages in a review to be printed in a newspaper or magazine.

Printed: March 2023

Published and Distributed By:
Lushena Books
607 Country Club Drive, Unit E
Bensenville, IL 60106
www.lushenabks.com

ISBN: 978-1-63923-932-0

TO MY MOTHER

IN RECOLLECTION OF THE YEARS WE PASSED TOGETHER IN EGYPT

I DEDICATE THIS BOOK

PREFACE.

THIS work, a reprint of articles on the Cities of Egypt mentioned in the Bible, has been written with the object of awaking such a popular interest in the famous sites described as may lead to their farther exploration. The Biblical notices of these cities, slight as they often are, have been chosen for their liveliness and human interest as the key-notes of each subject.

REGINALD STUART POOLE.

October 1882.

CONTENTS.

CHAPTER I.

INTRODUCTORY.

PAGE

Aspect of Egypt—True limits—Formation by Nile-deposit—
Names of Egypt and the Nile—Conflict of the Nile and the
desert: its place in Egyptian mythology—How the Hebrews
regarded Egypt and the desert 1

CHAPTER II.

MEMPHIS.

Necropolis alone remaining: its grandeur—Foundation of
city—Dyke of Menes—Names of Memphis—Religion
—Great temple: remains described by 'Abd-el-Lateef—
The Pyramid-field—belief of Egyptians in the future state
the cause of their costly tombs 15

CHAPTER III.

HANES.

Identity of Hanes with Heracleopolis proved by Mariette
—Religion of city—Heracleopolite Kings of Egypt: their
period a blank—Hanes in the time of the Assyrian Wars
—The Tablet of Naples—Need of exploration . . . 30

CHAPTER IV.

THEBES.

Splendid remains of city—Origin—Site — Names—Worship—History—Temple of El-Karnak: edifices on western bank: tombs 46

CHAPTER V.

ZOAN.

Historical importance of eastern border: its peculiar population—History of Zoan—The Shepherd Kings—The Hebrews—The Empire—Zoan rebuilt as Rameses—Shemite influence on Egyptian literature—Zoan during Oppression—Decline—Names—Religion—Description by an ancient Egyptian scribe—Ruins—Field for exploration 64

CHAPTER VI.

GOSHEN.

Local tradition as to Exodus untrue—Identification of city and land of Goshen—Local worship—Shemite colonists—History of Hebrew sojourn—Present state of the district and of the site of the capital 89

CHAPTER VII.

PITHOM.

Story of the Oppression of the Hebrews—Town of Pithom—Fragmentary Egyptian illustrations of the age—Brickmakers represented at Thebes—Shemite colonists in Goshen—Excavations would supply more information . 102

CHAPTER VIII.

MIGDOL.

route of the Exodus—Geological changes in Lower Egypt —Chain of lakes between the Mediterranean and the Red Sea—Migdol, the last camping-place, identified—Place where the Hebrews crossed—Dr. Brugsch's theory of the route 112

CHAPTER IX.

ON.

On, or Heliopolis, the Egyptian university—Origin —Names — Religious centre — The temple as described by the Ethiopian king Pianchi—History of city—Influence of the university on Alexandria—Teaching at Heliopolis— Its survival at Cairo—Remains of On—Tradition of visit of the Holy Family 131

CHAPTER X.

PI-BESETH.

I of city—Its great antiquity—Name and worship—Shishak and his family: record of his campaign in Palestine— Remains of temples—Festival of Bubastis—Historical character of Egyptian remains 150

CHAPTER XI.

SIN.

The approaches to Egypt--Strong position of Sin or Pelusium — Names—History—The Persian conquests of Egypt here

decided—The murder of Pompey at Pelusium—The site—
Historical lesson—Neighbouring stronghold Tahpanhes,
probably Daphnæ 166

CHAPTER XII.

ALEXANDRIA.

Foundation by Alexander—Plan—Advantages of situation—
Civil history : greatness under earlier Ptolemies : decline :
the Alexandrian mob—Alexandria as an intellectual centre :
worship of Sarapis : Museum and Library : faculties of university: extent of collections of books—Alexandrian philosophy: influence of Platonism seen in Egyptian temple : meeting of Greek and Hebrew thought: Platonism and Judaism :
Philo—Christianity at Alexandria—Influence of Platonism,
and action and reaction of Greek, Hebrew, and Egyptian
thought—Clement of Alexandria : Origen – Separation of
philosophers and churchmen: continued action of philosophy
on dogma : asceticism a gift of Egypt—Athanasius and
Arius : Julian : fall of paganism : fanaticism—Arab conquest—Scanty remains—Temple of Arsinoë and story of
Berenice's hair dedicated there—Farewell to Egypt . . 178

CHRONOLOGICAL SKETCH 211

NOTES 215

MAP.

Sketch Map to illustrate the Route of the ⎱ *To be placed between*
    Exodus . . . . ⎰ *pages* 120 *and* 121

CITIES OF EGYPT.

CHAPTER I.

INTRODUCTORY.

EGYPT is a land of light. The landscape lacks the charm of form, the majesty of the Alps, the solemn line of Atlas, the asperity of the Lycian crags which tower above the turbulent gulf of Adalia, the solid mass of snow-clad Lebanon, the pastoral softness of the Galilean hills. Plain and highland, meadow and forest, do not succeed one another as in those varied lands which are each a little world complete in itself. The colouring is monotonous. The fields change with the yearly course of nature or the threefold harvest which rewards the labour of man. The mountains of Egypt are white or yellow or tawny; on their rocky sides grows neither moss nor heather; no pines clothe their steep heights; no firs crown their level tops. The fields are varied alone by long avenues of stately palms in measured colonnades, or by the welcome shade of a rare sycamore. Nature does not transform the scene with a rain-storm or make it mysterious with vapours. There is neither rain nor cloud nor any mist. But those unvarying features are lighted up with ever-changing expression like a sympathetic face which takes its beauty from the influence of things around, reflecting pain or pleasure, joy or grief. Each day brings a rhythmic sequence of colour, from the moment when the long streaks of ruddy light in which Homer saw the rosy fingers of the Dawn begin to stretch across the eastern sky, until the olive after-glow reflects in its mirror the last rays of the sun fallen below the Libyan waste. But neither for the cloudless sunrise and sunset, nor for the herald of the one and the rear-guard of the other, does nature take most care. It is when the sun is in his strength and all he shines on is only relieved by the quivering of intense heat, a white heat as of a furnace, that the shadows are painted with sunset hues, and the sides of the barren mountains become luminous with liquid rose and purple and violet, like marvels of cloudland dropped on the earth. There are moments when we witness the same glow in the Greek islands, where the banished Apostle saw the Holy City descend from the skies in its splendour of sard and beryl, of sapphire and amethyst. At night the yellow glory of the moon walking in brightness makes but a softer day, or the deep blue sky of Egypt is lit up by many-coloured stars. The plague that foreshadowed the last and heaviest of all was the darkness that could be felt.

We must think of this strange beauty of Egypt if we would know why she has drawn to herself the Arab and the Hebrew from their life of freedom, and has yet a witchery for modern hearts, to prove the truth of the native saying that he who has drunk of the water of the Nile must return to drink of it again. We can see why the Egyptian has clung to his land with a love that is not patriotism, but a blind instinct of enjoyment, the sense of life that in the North wakens the world in spring alone. For all moves in harmony with nature, and existence is not without joy be the taskmaster's rod ever so heavy.

Egypt on the maps is not this wonderful land. We look and see a vast oblong space squared out in the north-eastern corner of Africa. This is a fiction of the geographers, as untrue to fact as the island Atlantis of Greek legend, or the Lyonesse of mediæval romance, both sunk beneath the ocean to explain their disappearance. The true Egypt of the old monuments, of the Hebrews, of the Greeks and Romans, of the Arabs, and of its own people in this day, is a mere fraction of this vast area of the maps, nothing more than the valley and plain watered by the Nile, for nearly seven hundred miles by the river's course from the Mediterranean southward. On either side are the great wastes, the highlands of the eastern desert, the undulating lowlands of the western, both parts of that great belt which runs across Africa and is nowhere broken but by the course of the Nile. The very populations are different. The scanty tribes which roam in the deserts are in manners, and some even in race, alien to the settled dwellers on the banks of the Nile. The strongest ruler of Egypt cannot call the wanderers his subjects. One tribe on the west moves from the Nile to the Atlantic. It would need a mighty Pharaoh to control the Benee 'Alee.

The story of Egypt is graven in its rocks, and written in its soil. Countless ages ago the mighty river gathered his forces in Central Africa, where the equatorial rains still yearly replenish a series of vast lakes. Forcing a way northward to lower levels, the mass of water cut a great trench in the rocky surface of the desert. In Upper Egypt this stupendous work is about three hundred feet deep from the top of the mountains to the river's bed, and from eight miles to less than a mile in breadth. As the Nile found a way to the sea, the waters sank to the base of the trench, leaving usually a level space on either side. With the rainy season of the equatorial region, the Nile still rises every year and carries northward the rich soil washed down from the highlands of Abyssinia, which with the beautiful regularity of nature is spread equally on the whole surface covered by the inundation, renewing the land, which never need lie fallow, nor have any artificial aid to make it fertile. This deposit has been carefully measured where in the course of centuries it has risen up the sides of monuments of known date. The rate of increase is only about four inches and a half in a century, yet this is amply enough to fertilize the land. Near Cairo the trench of the Nile-valley opens out into a great triangular plain, the Delta, or Lower Egypt, won, like all deltas, from the ocean. Two great branches of the river water it, following its outline. This vast surface, formed of successive deposits, shows how much of the gift of the Nile man suffers to be yearly poured away into the sea and lost for ever. Were a cutting made anywhere from the river into the desert, the stream would carry Egypt with it in its course. No sooner was the Freshwater Canal cut and the waters of the Nile admitted, than the wilderness bloomed with mysterious herbage.

The natural division into valley and plain, and the character of Egypt, give us a clue to the names of the country. In the older books of the Bible we find Mizraim a dual word, the two Mazors, like the two Sicilies. In the Prophets Mazor sometimes occurs, and even Mizraim for the Delta, while Pathros is their name for Upper Egypt, the native Pa-ta-res, the Southland. The derivation of Mazor is obscure, and conjecture is mere learned idling; but it is interesting to know that the old name survives in Misr, in the vulgar speech Masr, the Arabic name of Egypt, and strangely also of its capital. The old Egyptians do not leave us in doubt as to their definition of their country; with them it was 'Kem,' the 'Black,' from the colour of its soil: there is no place for the yellow desert in this descriptive name.

The last use of Kem died out in the form Chemi in Coptic, the descendant of the classical language, which ceased to be spoken a century ago. It survives among us in the terms 'chemistry' and 'alchemy,' sciences thought to be of Egyptian origin.

The Greek name which is the parent of our Egypt is as obscure in its meaning as Mazor. We first find it in the Homeric poems. In the Odyssey, it seems strangely used for both country and river, only changing the gender from feminine to masculine. There may be sound reason in this. Once a year, when the fertilising flood covers the whole valley and plain, river and country are one, from desert to desert. This ancient use of the name of Egypt ceases with Homer: thenceforward, the stream is called the Nile.

Still more fit than the names of Egypt are those of the Nile. The modern people call it 'the sea,' an Arab way of speaking of the mightiest rivers; and with them 'the Nile' means the inundation. Nahum, when he warns Nineveh, telling her how the Assyrian sacked her rival and ancient conqueror Thebes, calls the water-rampart of the Egyptian capital, not the river, but 'the sea' (Nah. iii. 8). The usual Hebrew name is 'the river,' 'yeôr,' but this is not the common word for river. It is a special one almost reserved for the Nile and the canals it feeds. A rarer name in Hebrew is Shichôr, 'the black,' and we also find 'the river of Mizraim' where the common Hebrew word for 'river' is used. Nile, the Greek name, seems to mean 'dark blue' or 'black.' We may compare it to Shichôr and to the modern Bahr-el-Azrak, or 'Blue Sea,' as the great stream which brings down the fertilising soil to Egypt is now called, while its rival is the Bahr-el-Abyad, or 'White Sea.' The Nile in Egypt is never clear, and its volume and depth give it the deep hue which Shichôr and Nile describe; for the vagueness of antiquity has not our fine sense of the tones of colour.

The mystery of the source of the Nile struck the fancy of the old Egyptians. Hence the sacred name Hapi, 'the Hidden,' under which the river was worshipped as a god.

Not, however, in this form does the Nile take high rank in the Egyptian religion: Hapi is only the river personified, the fruitful genius who with his water-plants builds up the throne of Pharaoh. In a larger sense the Nile is identified with Osiris, 'the good being,' the source of light and plenty, thus at once the sun and the Nile. As the sun, Osiris ruled not only the world of light, but also, and more specially, the world of darkness. He was the sun of the night, the ruler of the shades. Each Egyptian took his name after death, that as Osiris he might conquer darkness and return in light.

As the Nile, Osiris is the hidden source of fertility and nourishment, in perpetual warfare with barrenness and famine. His enemy was Set, whom the Greeks called Typhon, the desert, the sea, the storm, darkness, and destruction. The force of this opposition lies in the contrast of the desert to Egypt. Take one step from the valley or plain, rich with teeming vegetation, full of life, and you are at once in a waste utterly barren and dead, whether it be the mountainous region on the east or the rolling stretch of lowland on the west. There are the marks of a perpetual conflict; here the Nile has won for Egypt a new strip of the desert, there the sand has poured in and obliterated the fertile land. No wonder that the Egyptians saw in this the war of good and evil. No wonder that in another and gentler sense the western expanse, to them illimitable, impassable, mysterious, wherein the sun daily sank and disappeared, became the region of death, the symbol of 'God's underworld,' 'the hidden land,' 'the West, the ancient, the perfect, the vast.'

It is in such figures as these, in the use of an epithet, in the natural expression of surprise or pleasure or awe, that the ancients show us their sense of nature in terse utterances whose force puts to shame our modern attempts to picture in words. Thus the sudden view of the plain of the Delta as its green expanse refreshes the eye wearied with the monotony of the parched yellow desert is brought before us in a single sentence. The plain of Jordan ere it was blasted was 'well watered everywhere,' 'as the garden of the Lord, like the land of Egypt, as thou comest unto Zoan' (Gen. xiii. 10).[1]

After the long and bitter bondage Egypt did not always wear this pleasant colour to the Hebrew eye. It had a Janus face. It was the land of plenty where they had eaten freely the abundant and varied produce of the earth, the land of kindly folk who did not share in the stern policy of their rulers, and had always a welcome

[1] Zoan for Zoar here seems the better reading, unless we may suppose Zal or Zar, the Egyptian name of Zoan, to be meant: Zoar of Palestine can scarcely be intended, for the passage would then be unlike the simple style of Genesis.

INTRODUCTORY.

for the fugitive from Palestine ; but it was also the house of bondage, where as in a furnace of iron they had toiled under the burning sun, while the taskmaster smote their bare shoulders with a continual stroke. The meaner souls, as they grew weary of the wilderness or waxed feeble in the struggle for existence against Canaanite and Assyrian, could not forget the flesh-pots of Egypt. The runaway Saneha, whose adventures are preserved in a papyrus roll, when he tells us in the story of his flight how he wandered on the border faint and hungry, measures his progress by the Egyptian supper-time.

To the land of plenty the Hebrew and the Arab have always fled when their pastures have been smitten by drought. Rarely have they come in vain. For there can be no dearth in Egypt unless the river fail, and this is most unusual. Thus the regular rise of the Nile came to be expected, and was no doubt ascribed by the people to the river-god, rather than to the Divine Ruler of all things. Perhaps this tendency struck the native poet who in his beautiful hymn to the Nile makes the genius of the river a manifestation of the hidden divinity who cannot be graven by the sculptor, unseen, whom no offering reaches, who cannot be drawn to the mysteries, his place unknown, whom no abode can hold, whose mind none can attain unto. Yet to this day the river is reverenced. Every year before the festal ceremony of cutting the canal of Cairo, the signal that the inundation has attained its needed height,- a pillar of mud is raised to be washed away by the rising waters : it is called 'the bride,' and legend says that it represents a virgin who in ancient times was decked in gay apparel and cast into the stream as a sacrifice, by a fiercer marriage than that in which the Doge of Venice was wont to wed the Adriatic. We see another indication that the common people did not look beyond the Nile to Providence, in the contrast drawn in Deuteronomy between the husbandry of Egypt and that of Palestine, the mechanical nature of the one, the faith that watched the varying seasons in the other (Deut. xi. 10–12).

The wonderful spectacle of Egypt flooded by the inundation, the Delta one vast lake, a torrent between desert and desert, in the valley of Upper Egypt, towns and villages islanded in the swirling waters, the people hurrying their cattle to places of safety—this sight, welcome as it is to the natives, is full of terror to the stranger. Thus the Hebrew prophets, writing in days when the memory of the sojourn had passed away, take the Nile in flood-time as a figure for the onrush of a mighty army of invasion (Jer. xlvi. 7, 8), and also for utter destruction when a land is swept clean of its inhabitants (Amos ix. 5).

The desert-like Egypt had a twofold aspect to the Hebrews as it has to all who have since known it. To the wayfarer it is terrible in its loneliness, its vastness, its silence, its lack of all that makes the earth pleasant to the eye with signs of life and verdure, with offer of food and water. It is a dry and thirsty land, and that means more than all the rest when the sun beats with unremitting force till the earth is as heated iron beneath a sky of molten brass. Yet it had another face. There have always been those who chose the desert life because they desired to leave mankind for a time to be alone with God. Abraham preferred the border of the desert to the pleasant plain of Jordan. Moses fled to the desert for those many years in which he prepared to be the leader and lawgiver. Elijah went to Horeb when he would solve the question whether he was indeed the last of the faithful. In the desert the Baptist passed his early days, until the voice crying in the wilderness peopled the waste with those who came from busy city and field to repent in its solemn quiet. The old Egyptian hermits founded in the desert the hardest monastic state, which surrendered all the joys of life in exchange for the calm of the silent valleys. For in those tremendous solitudes there is neither sight nor sound to disturb the mind. In the mighty rocks and the rolling hills, stretching far away to immeasurable distance, not clothed by nature, untrod by man, save in the rare tracks where his timorous uncertain footprints are washed away by the first light air that stirs the sand, under the luminous heavens, most of all when the night has fallen, more than even in the midst of the ocean, man seems conscious of the Divine Presence. Nothing is between him and the heavens which open their portals wide. The world need not be shut out, with its changing shows, its restless movement, its many voices of to-day : it is so far away that it is as though it had never been. The scene which through countless ages has known no change is full of the silence and the rest of eternity.

CHAPTER II.

MEMPHIS.

No one of the great cities of the old world has so utterly disappeared as Memphis. Her rival Thebes has yet four splendid temples to attest the greatness which Homer sang. Babylon and Nineveh are still marked by vast mounds, the sepulchres of their treasures. Athens nestles, as of yore, beneath her ancient citadel of rock. Rome has endured for six-and-twenty centuries the storms of changing fortune, and is growing once more. Jerusalem, long shrunken within her first limits of near three thousand years ago, is again enlarging herself. But no temple or town attests the former wealth of Memphis, or preserves a fragment of her once abounding life. There is neither sacred building, nor palace, nor a trace of common houses, nothing to show where the long ramparts rose, or where the White Wall, the ancient citadel, defended the capital. The mighty city, which for three, four, or five thousand years was first or second in Egypt; the famous shrine, enriched by successive kings, from the first who ruled the land to the Macedonian sovereigns who courted the powerful priesthood; all that stood within the ample circuit of the walls, is levelled to the ground, and the traveller is shown a fallen Colossus[1] and a few fragments near by, and told that he stands in the precincts of the Temple of Ptah, the Egyptian Vulcan, and that of Memphis herself nothing else remains.

Yet no city in the world has so many or such costly monuments. As you stand on the platform of the Citadel of Cairo that commands the westward view, you look across the vast modern city, the plantations of mulberry trees and the rolling Nile, and the other side of the valley rich in corn-lands, with the long line of palms in which Memphis is just traced, and you see in the farthest distance the low edge of the Libyan desert, spreading like an even rampart, along whose summit rise in four groups the shining masses of the Pyramids of Memphis, like the boundary-marks of the mighty waste,

[1] The Colossus is said to have been recently set up by an English traveller.

the Egyptian land of the shades, the abode of the sun after his setting. The city of the living has perished, the city of the dead remains, remains with the royal sepulchres, and around them the humbler tombs of subjects, sculptured and inscribed with the lively records of what was done in the remote past by those whose mummies have crumbled to dust in the lapse of ages. Memphis the lost is here recovered. We may walk through the silent streets of the City of the Dead, as did the hero of an old Egyptian romance, and read the writings that are engraven on the outer walls of the tombs, and we shall not listen to the words of any one who, like the magician who accosted him, shall tell us our interest is profitless. For we have discovered the true magic in the recovery of the records of the past, in giving speech to the long-silent utterances of the hopes and fears, the joys and sorrows of the fathers of mankind, who return from the underworld and admit us to their company, as, having interpreted the title without, we can enter each sepulchral chapel and understand when and why and for whom its pictured reliefs were made in olden time.

The foundation of Memphis is the first event in

Egyptian history, the one large historical incident in the reign of the first king, who emerges a real man from the shadowland which the Egyptians called the reign of the gods. Let us try and span in our minds the vast interval which has passed since the days of Menes. Look once more with me from the Citadel of Cairo westward, and beneath our feet is spread out the greatest of Eastern cities, Masr the Victorious, splendid yet with the fast-decaying mosques of the Moslem rule, so numerous that they foil the attempt to count them. In a series of successive styles, the Eastern counterparts of the changes of Western art, you pass in time through the base art of the Turkish rule, to group after group, or memorial after memorial, up to the earliest and greatest of all, whose vast court, surrounded by colonnades with pointed arches, marks the first stage in Arab art. A thousand years have passed since it was built. Two centuries more take us to the Arab conquest. This art, nobly massive or delicately sumptuous, has passed through its phases since, while the like changes have worked in the hearts and minds of men, while race after race, dynasty after dynasty, has ruled over Egypt. Yet this is but a mere fragment of the time since Menes reigned. Memphis was in her decay when the Arabs poured into the country, and soon ceased to be a town. She had lived before as the second city of Egypt through the Roman and the Greek dominion; she had been taken by the Persian and the Assyrian and the Ethiopian. We go back to the dawn of Greek history, farther yet to the Exodus when Israel became a nation, and still we have not reached the age of the supremacy of Memphis. Still earlier, before Abraham, we attain at last the long unmeasured period of the six great lines of Egyptian kings who ruled at Memphis, and were buried in the Pyramids that overlook her obliterated site. The space of time from our days to the starting-point of Egyptian history we cannot measure. Authorities differ by some two thousand years. But numbers make no clear impression. It is far more striking to note the movements of history, not in Egypt alone, but outside its limits, and to remember that the existence of religions, the sway of empires, and the rule of races, have taken up but fragments of this vast interval.

Menes, or Mena, the first mortal king, who stands at the head of our uncounted reckoning of time, leader of the roll of thirty dynasties which filled the list of Manetho the native annalist,—Menes, the founder of Memphis and Egyptian history, came from the south. Civilisation descended the Nile. His native place was Thinis, or This, in Upper Egypt, a still older town, where his shadowy predecessors ruled. He united under his single sway 'the two regions' of Egypt, and at once erected a new capital, from which he could control the whole country. The site was happily chosen, and neither the glory of Thebes nor the traffic of Alexandria ever took away the seat of government for long—for a few centuries only in each case—from the neighbourhood of the oldest capital. It was well called 'the balance of the two regions.' Where the valley of Upper Egypt is about to spread out into the plain of the Delta, a strong city could rule both, and hold the entrance of the narrow Upper Country, the first of many barriers which could stay the advance of the invader, and so give courage to a retiring army.

The marvel of the origin of Memphis lies in the work that went before. Here in the beginnings of history we picture to ourselves a rude people, whose primitive collection of huts grew to be a city. But it was not so. A great engineering work was the first act of the builder.

He chose his site, and then boldly fought the Nile, and turned the mighty river from his course. The site pleased him, but the stream was on the wrong side, flowing below the Libyan chain, flowing over where the city should be, offering no water-bulwark against the invader from the eastern border. So he raised, a few miles to the south, a mighty dyke, and turned the river into the present course, founding the city on the west bank, in the rich valley, with the desert behind and the Nile before. The dyke can no longer be traced, but it was known to the Greeks as the work of Menes. But how are we sure that the tradition is true? The dyke was there, and Memphis stands in the former bed of the river. If Menes did not turn the stream, the dyke must have been a still earlier work.

Such an enterprise is one of the most difficult that man can attempt; for you may stop or divert a stream, but if you would do lasting work, you have to struggle with gigantic forces, and the larger, the more rapid, and the more varying in height the river, the greater your risks of failure. Yet this work of skill meets us on the threshold of Egyptian history. It contradicts our notions of the gradual rise of the nation. It accords with the effect the Pyramids produce on our mind, themselves not much later than the age of Menes.

The new city received a name which reflects the satisfaction of the ancient founder; he called it Mennufre, 'the Good' or 'Perfect Mansion.' This was the civil name: like the other towns of Egypt, it had a sacred name, denoting its local worship, 'the House' or 'Abode of Ptah.' The citadel was not raised on a hill to overawe the townsfolk; it was merely the oldest quarter, the primitive city, girt with a strong rampart of the light yellow limestone afforded by the neighbouring desert, and washed on one side by the river,—'the White Wall.' The civil name is the parent of the Greek Memphis and the Hebrew Moph, also found in the form Noph. Lately, scholars have thought that the famous capital of Ethiopia, the royal seat of Tirhakah, the classical Napata and Egyptian Nap, is intended by Noph. But in favour of the older opinion here adopted is the ready interchange of the initial letters in Hebrew, and the unlikelihood that but a single notice should occur in the prophets of the great city of Egypt of their days. To them it must have been what Cairo now is to the dwellers in Palestine, the centre of Egyptian power and wealth;

if then rivalled by Thebes, it was nearest to the border, and known better to the merchant and the fugitive, the bourne to which politicians turned their longing eyes, while the prophets warned them in vain. If we bear this in mind, the notices better suit the northern city than remote Napata. Ethiopia was far beyond the Hebrew horizon, and is rather mentioned as a power coming from the south than, as the Egyptians knew it, a country with its cities and temples, a farther Egypt that discovery has restored to the light from its long oblivion.

Memphis was the Abode of Ptah, the Egyptian Vulcan, not the metal-worker, as Greeks and Romans imagined him, but the divine artificer, the creative power. His name most strangely is Semitic, or in other words Hebrew. Two classes of such words are found in Egyptian, one as old as the language itself, the first gift of the East, the other borrowed about the time of Moses, when it was the fashion to mix as many Semitic words as possible in the spoken language, as we and the Germans have done with French. The name of Ptah is of the old stock; and finding so early an Eastern visitor, we are inclined to ask whether the idea of which he is the centre, the notion of creation, came into Egypt from the East.

The temple of Ptah, founded by Menes, grew, with the costly additions of later kings to the main edifice, and the new structures they built around it. Here must have been a long line of tablets, inscriptions, statues, and sphinxes, records of victory and proofs of subjugation, all, like the successive works of a great cathedral, in an order which told their historic sequence, unlike them each inscribed with the names of the kings and great men who ordered them to be graven. Here stood the statue of king Sethos, the priest of Ptah, set up to commemorate the destruction of Sennacherib. All are gone but the broken Colossus of the great Ramses, the oppressor of Israel, and a few fragments around. The false gods have ceased out of Noph (*see* Ezek. xxx. 13).

Very different was the aspect which the ancient site presented to the learned Arabian physician, philosopher, and traveller, Abd-el-Lateef of Baghdad, who visited Egypt about the beginning of the thirteenth century. The beauty of the remains of the chief temple and its surroundings struck him with wonder; the great monolithic shrine of breccia verde, nine cubits high, eight long, and seven broad, the doors which swung on hinges of stone, the well-carven statues, the lions terrific in their aspect; and he praises those former kings who took care that these monuments should be preserved, and forbad their injury or wanton destruction, although they were hostile to those who made them. He adds four reasons for 'the protection of ancient buildings:' first, because they afford records for the reckoning of time; secondly, because they bear witness to the truth of the Kurán, relating the history to which reference is there made; thirdly, because they admonish us whence we come and whither we must return (pointing out the fate of our predecessors); fourthly, because they display the condition of ancient peoples, their mode of life, the abundance of their learning, and the exactness of their thought;—all which matters incite the mind to desire fuller knowledge. He then contrasts the license and cupidity of his time, and portrays the treasure-seekers demolishing the beautiful works of antiquity in their fruitless search.

His protest was in vain. The desire for treasure gave way to the desire for building materials. The sultáns and princes of Cairo found in Memphis a ready quarry; the green monolith was demolished, and column after column carried away for the mosques and palaces of the latest rival of Memphis. A reaction of bigotry added a fresh motive; and the wise counsels of the old philosopher, who claimed historical monuments as confirmations of the truth, found no favour with those who ignorantly made a merit of destroying the records of idolatry.

Thus has Memphis been carried away. Yet the great necropolis still remains on the edge of the desert behind, stretching north and south nearly twenty miles, with its populous centres behind the city, its smaller suburbs far away, marked by above sixty pyramids, some nearly perfect, some in ruins, the greatest still preserving their first shape when seen from afar. These are the royal tombs; around them, ranged in streets, are the sepulchres of subjects, some massively built of stone, others cut in the sides of the rock, where its form allowed, others again mere pits leading to chambers of sepulture. The subterranean tomb of the sacred bull Apis is a stupendous excavation, mainly a series of grand galleries, from which open out chambers, each large enough to hold the massive sarcophagus of a mummied bull.

The vast extent of this city of the dead is some measure of the long duration of Egyptian history.

Most of the many pyramids are the tombs of kings, and all these belong to the earliest line, that of the Memphite sovereigns whose power ended before the time of Abraham. The rest of the tombs are of many dates; some ages are fully represented, some are without records, as if another great burial-place had come into favour. Even with these gaps, the accumulation is unequalled. The Chaldæan city of Erech, the modern Warka, alone approaches Memphis as a necropolis; but the quantity and the character of the sepultures is quite insignificant in comparison. The extent of the desert which is occupied by the ancient Egyptian cemetery, and the costliness of the tombs, have no parallel elsewhere. No wonder that the Israelites, as they saw Pharaoh in pursuit, thought of the burial-grounds of Egypt, when in irony they said to Moses, 'Because (there were) no graves in Egypt, hast thou taken us away to die in the wilderness?' (Exod. xiv. 11), while with a more pointed reference to the great necropolis, Hosea predicts of the Israelite fugitives, 'Egypt shall gather them up, Moph shall bury them' (Hosea ix. 6).

The consequence thus given to the tomb by an active and joyous people is at first perplexing. We must think of them as the only nation of the times before later Judaism and Christianity who had a vital belief in the future state. To the Egyptian all he did on earth was sure to bring him happiness or misery hereafter. He was to be judged according to his actions, acquitted or condemned by the unerring test of truth. This noble doctrine became in a measure corrupted by a system of elaborate prayers and incantations, which would substitute the paid acts of the priesthood and magical rites for a life led by the dictates of conscience or, as the Egyptians would say, the heart. Still the sense of the importance of the hereafter was never lost. Closely bound up with this feeling was the desire to preserve the body. It may be doubted if they believed it would rise, but it must repose deep beneath the sepulchral chapel, that there, on each festival, the kinsfolk might resort to say the prayers for the dead. The chapel was necessary for the soul's welfare, and the mummy connected the worship there with the identity of the deceased. Moreover, the estates were taxed for the services of the chapel, and thus the mummy became a kind of title-deed, securing the estates to his descendants so long as the dues were paid to the priests who served the chapel. But this was accidental. The Egyptian tomb was due to no mere convention; faith raised its mighty mass above the rock or cut its hidden halls beneath. Those who accuse this great nation of a vain ostentation in these costly sepulchres, cannot conceive the delight of lavishing gold and silver without return in the commemoration of a noble idea. The Egyptians raised monuments that have defied time, to show [to all who should come after them that they believed in the immortality of the soul.

CHAPTER III.

HANES.

THERE are cities and men whom we meet but once in written history. Some of them appear abruptly without geographical place or note of descent, mere names to us and nothing more. They shine for a moment out of the darkness of the past and are lost. If we are careful readers, desirous to understand, we open some dictionary and follow our will-o'-the-wisps into a morass peopled by the strange creations of the commentators. What were names easily forgotten become riddles impossible to remember. Suddenly some ancient monument, a tablet, a statue, or a coin, newly dug out of the earth, recalls the lost word and clothes it with all the circumstance of historical reality; it becomes at once a living thing, and we marvel how it could ever have been a dead symbol.

Such has been the fate of the city of Hanes, once

only mentioned in the Bible. In the days of the supreme struggle with Assyria, Hebrew ambassadors went thither to beg for Egyptian aid. 'His princes were at Zoan, and his ambassadors came to Hanes' (Isa. xxx. 4). The envoys passed on their fruitless errand through the terrible wilderness, their beasts laden with costly presents (vers. 5-7). As we read we recognise Zoan, the great frontier-town, the seat in that time of the Pharaoh who enjoyed the right of descent from an earlier line that claimed supremacy. The position of Zoan is fixed in the Bible. Does not the name mean 'the place of departure,' where the caravans left the last great town of Egypt behind and were soon to enter on the desert way? Was not Goshen hard by? Zoan stands out prominent in Egyptian history, like the mighty ruins which mark her desolate site, from which the story of forgotten ages has been recovered for these later times. But what and where was Hanes? The Greek translators of the Old Testament, labouring in Egypt, could not tell, the patient Chaldees who paraphrased the Scripture in the vulgar tongue of Palestine could not tell. Gesenius, that prince of modern Hebrew scholars, guessed that Hanes must be the city which the Copts called Hnes, the Greeks Heracleopolis, the town of Hercules, one the civil, the other the religious name. No hint of history confirmed the conjecture, which rested on the likeness of a word of three Hebrew letters to another of four Coptic ones. And the Greek translators did not read it in the Hebrew text from which they translated. So Gesenius was not convincing, and Hanes remained a blank to the reader and a plaything for the critics.

Research on the spot is better than study at home, more especially when study has no materials to work withal. It is hard to make bricks without straw, but who can build without bricks? Solid as they seem, the old tomes of antiquarian research, now left to idle curiosity and the industrious bookworm, are mere phantoms, airy constructions that could only live in the dead calm of indifference. The breath of inquiry has blown them away. We now know that it is worse than useless to speculate where we can observe, to theorise when we have only to reach out our hands and grasp the facts. So in the great centres of antique civilisation people are beginning to scratch the ground, here uncovering a wall, there clearing a chamber, in the temples and palaces of

Egypt and Assyria. It may be that we shall even dig in earnest, could a little money but be spared from the pressing claims of show, and luxury, and folly, for labours which are certain of their reward, if we dare but exchange a lottery which is all blanks for a lottery which is all prizes. The cost of a pack of hounds would in a few years clear all the monuments of Egypt. Sennacherib was a mighty hunter, but he found time for literary work, and organised research that the records of former times should be preserved for the times to come.

Mariette, the great explorer of Egypt, whose loss we still deplore, with small funds and in the teeth of endless difficulties, by stern determination and the gallant spirit of a Frenchman, achieved more than all who had gone before him. He has fallen at last in the fight, killed by overwork and difficulties, but not by failure; failure he refused to recognise. To him we owe the answer to many a riddle of the mysterious Sphinx, all but the Sphinx's own riddle of origin and purpose. At his bidding buried cities have thrown off the grave-clothes which had enwrapped them for thousands of years, and risen to tell us their story, and to fill the ages of oblivion once more with the joy of overflowing life. He had the peculiar instinct, the magic power, to know where the precious metal lay beneath his feet. Wherever you uncover the ground in any Egyptian site you find some buried record, a tablet, or a bronze : on the very surface lie the potsherds on which the schoolboys wrote out precious fragments of what were classics in the days of Moses : all are treasures, but of varying worth. Genius alone can discriminate, leaving the dross, content with nothing less than pure gold. So Mariette, not satisfied with the whole field of Egyptian research, bethought him of Ethiopia, and thus left all Lower Nubia untouched and sent his explorers across the desert in which the army of Cambyses perished, to the far-off southland, where under the sacred mountain rises the temple of Napata, the capital of Tirhakah, greatest of Ethiopian kings. Here he knew he would find records of that royal line who stood for a while against all the might of Assyria, the heroes of the great conflict for world-dominion, in the tumult of which the kingdom of Israel disappeared for ever. Nor was the adventurous explorer disappointed. Tablet after tablet rewarded the search. Of all these the most weighty, though not the most curious, was the famous stele of Pianchi, which tells the story how Egypt was conquered by this king of Ethiopia, about a generation before Isaiah. From this record we learn that in those days the long-undivided kingdom had broken up into many small states. Zoan was then the seat of that Pharaoh who represented earlier kings who claimed to rule all Egypt, while Chenensu, the Hanes of Scripture and Heracleopolis of the Greeks, was ruled by a powerful lesser king. This little episode of discovery is a fitting prelude to the history of the long-forgotten town.

The site of Hanes is one which has never been touched by the explorer. The traveller who sails up the Nile is unattracted by its mounds. Are not these brown masses which cover each of them the history of an ancient city far too numerous not to be passed by? They may claim a moment's notice if some famous name like Saïs or Bubastis is attached to them in the map, and lingers like an echo of the past in the name of the squalid modern village, that clings to a corner of the ample space once crowded with the homes of plenty. If you land, you find one poor street, in which are sold the commonest Manchester cottons and the yet inferior work of the Egyptian looms, where once the fine linen of Egypt and the gold and ivory of Ethiopia were bartered against the embroidery of the East, dyed with Tyrian purple, and the splendid metal-work of the Phœnician craftsmen. The wealth of antiquity, historical as well as material, lies deep below your feet in the layers of successive habitations.

Before his end, when he knew the hand of death was upon him, Mariette, hitherto reticent of his secret, even to the extent of what some called jealousy, though the motive must have been the desire to exclude the ignorant and the reckless from his mines of antiquity, the year before last, the great explorer made his will, appointing the learned world at once his executor and legatee. In a memoir, summing up all that he knew was most urgent, he stated to the French Academy of Inscriptions, who have published the document, what may be called the claim of Egyptian exploration on the interest of Europe. He left nothing untold in this memorable paper, with a full trust that refutes the charge of jealousy. One of the leading works he there proposed is the excavation of Hanes.

Hanes lay in the most favoured part of Middle

Egypt. Hitherto we have spoken of Upper and Lower Egypt only, the narrow valley and the wide plain. This is the great natural division, and at all times it has been the most usual. But Upper Egypt is again roughly parted by nature into a broader and a narrower valley. The Heptanomis, or region of the seven provinces or nomes, the northernmost part, is far broader and more productive than the Thebaïs, which takes its name from Thebes, the southernmost district. In the Heptanomis, about seventy miles by the river above Cairo, on the western bank, stood the city of Hanes. The site is marked by the extensive mounds around the Arab village of Ahnás-el-Medeeneh, 'Ahnás the capital,' a name probably preserving the remembrance that in earlier times this was the chief town of a province. Our knowledge of its history is wholly due to literary sources, Egyptian and classical. From the Egyptian we learn that it was the seat of the worship of Hershefiu, the Egyptian Hercules. His name means 'the vigorous,' or 'strong,' and this is why the Greeks call him Hercules, thinking of their personification of bodily strength. The two have no true connection. The Greek idea travelled from Assyria, and as it took form in the curious works in gold and silver and bronze that the Phœnicians carried to the islands of Greece, it gained the shapes we well know, first the slayer of the Lion and the Hydra, ending at last in the boxer with his swollen ears, the coarse ideal of a depraved age. The Egyptian god of strength was portrayed with a ram's head, by that strange union in which animal worship and a higher idolatry met. This divinity was a local form of Chnum the creator, who is represented moulding the world as a potter on his wheel. His force is thus creative, not combative. No remains of the temple at Heracleopolis are known: doubtless they are hidden beneath the rubbish in the centre of the mounds. Sacred buildings are always to be sought in depressions, for while the houses of age after age rose as the ruins of each period elevated the mounds, the temples always retained their primitive site, and all the additions and restorations stood on the first level of their sacred precincts.

It is not, however, for the curious details of the tangled mythology of Egypt alone that search should be made at Hanes. Temple and town, and the unknown necropolis that must lie in the Libyan waste, should be excavated for the materials of a lost book of history.

For here ruled two ancient dynasties of kings at the second capital of Egypt.

Six royal lines held sway at Memphis, and the Pyramids and lesser tombs around preserve their history. 'The Sixth Dynasty,' says Mariette in the memoir which is his legacy to knowledge, 'had scarcely closed when there suddenly appears in the series of monuments a deep gap which does not end until the accession of the first king of the Eleventh Dynasty, four hundred and thirty-six years later.' 'This is a sort of chasm where, in no part of Egypt, does a tablet, a statue, a tomb, not the smallest fragment, show itself, during near four centuries and a half.' The very duration of time is doubtful, and no royal name of the Egyptian hieroglyphic lists can be assigned to any one of the four dynasties of the interval. The native historian Manetho only says that the first two of these were of Memphis, the second two of Heracleopolis, and that the founder of the kingdom of Hanes was Achthoes, a cruel tyrant worse than all his predecessors, who did evil to all the people of Egypt, until at length he went mad, and was killed by a crocodile. This is the sole fragment of the history of centuries lying between two luminous periods. These

Memphites and Heracleopolites, in their obscurity, are very uninteresting. Who cares to pierce the darkness? Yet they lie between the men who built the greatest wonders of the world, the Pyramids, which are still the subjects of the romance of science, and those greater sovereigns who conquered nature and did a work of engineering skill, in making the Lake Mœris, an enterprise unrivalled in Egypt. Supposing we had no history, neither chronicler nor charter, no monuments, neither cathedral nor castle, between William the Conqueror and Henry VII.,—how curiously should we look into the blank abyss, wondering how the people fared, what kings ruled, what law controlled, what faith prevailed; yet Egypt in this dark time had her kings, her laws, and her religion. As with us, so with those who drank the waters of the Nile, the mighty work of progress moved, and if it seemed arrested, yet again went on the faster. And were we shown a mound somewhere in the heart of England, and told that there our lost kings had their royal seat, should we grudge a few thousand pounds to restore the pedigree of the nation, to recover the lost decades of our Livy? Yet Mariette has pointed to Ahnás-el-Medeeneh, and told us that there we must strive to bring to life the long-lost records of the kings whose royal seat it was, but as yet has spoken in vain.

The fall of the kingdom of Hanes dates long before the days of Abraham. Thousands of years pass by and the city has no place in history, only is its worship mentioned here and there in the religious records. The life of the Hebrew race from Abraham to Joseph, the sojourn of four hundred and thirty years, the age of the Judges, the empire of David and Solomon, all pass by—what a measure of time is this!—and two hundred years yet later, in the last conflict of the Israelite kingdom, the old capital reappears as a seat of royalty.

This age, when the portentous figure of the Assyrian darkened the East, was a time of confusion. Egypt, like a vast Colossus resting on a sandy foundation, had fallen prone, and broken into fragments. The wide dominions of Solomon had divided into a crowd of rival kingdoms. All countries seemed to be resolved into their first elements, Egypt perhaps most of all. For Egypt was a collection of small states, each with a distinctive variety of religion of its own, bound together by the strong will of a central government, that bond once broken, able each to stand alone. Four leading kings thus disputed for supremacy. At Zoan ruled a pageant sovereign, maybe he to whom the Hebrew envoys made their weary journey, a man who had prestige enough to negotiate for them, not vigour enough to act. At Hanes a scion of the line of Shishak held his court. A brother king to the south was of more pretension to the first place. On the west a wary patriot, Tafnecht of Saïs, dared to lead the popular party, which at last won its way after a struggle which engages all our sympathy. Necho and Hophra were his descendants. But, more powerful than all, the representative of the priest-kings of Thebes ruled from Napata all Ethiopia and southern Egypt, and, called in by his partisans, met and conquered the Saïte and his allies. This is the story which Pianchi, the conqueror, tells in his famous tablet. The prince of Hanes had been forced into the Saïte alliance, and on its defeat he made his submission 'with tributes to Pharaoh,' such as the Hebrew envoys brought when they came to the ancient city, 'gold, silver, and all precious stones, with steeds the choicest of his stud.' His little state lingered on, and one of his successors is found as a tributary of the Assyrian king Assur-ban-habal, some eighty years later. Soon after it must have fallen, when the Saïte supremacy was at last finally won, and the little kingdoms that had worn away Egypt with their jealousies abolished, by the strong hand of Psametik, the father of Necho.

Once more does Hanes reappear in history. In the Museum of Naples there is a curious votive tablet of an Egyptian priest. He had obeyed the Persians and gone to Asia in their service. He thanks Chnum, of whom we recollect the god of Hanes to have been a form. 'Thou didst protect me,' he says, 'in the war of the Greeks, when thou didst repel Asia.' The subject then changes. The Egyptian priest has been present at one of the great battles, either when Alexander crossed the Granicus, or at the decisive field of Issus or of Arbela. He is still in Asia, but he is called back by Chnum, who commands him to go to Hanes, and alone he traverses the ocean.[1] So from the Ionian or the

[1] This tablet has been differently translated, in part by Dr. Brugsch, and fully by the late Mr. Goodwin. (*Records of the Past*, iv., 65 foll.) On careful examination of the text, Dr. Brugsch's views, generally adopted above, seem correct. It is curious that the old priest mentions a king of Persia, but not by name, nor does he name the Greek conqueror. Perhaps his record belongs to the interval during which the Persian Empire was falling, but before Alexander had received the submission of Egypt.

Cilician coast the old patriot made his way to the north of Egypt, it may be while yet the route along Phœnicia was unsafe, and sailed up one of the branches of the Nile until at length he reached Hanes, and recorded in thankfulness his double escape by land and by sea. This tablet, set up, it may be, there, gives us the last glimpse of the city in the old Egyptian times.

Under the Copts and Arabs Hanes still remained. A Muslim writer tells us how in its neighbourhood there was a convent, on the banks of the Nile, called the Monastery of Light. Its church was dedicated to the archangel Gabriel. The donjon had six very lofty stages, and was of beautiful architecture. Around the convent was a circular wall, and in its circuit four hundred fruitful date-palms. The convent has disappeared, at least from the maps. Search should be made for its ruins, for no doubt it was built of materials quarried from Egyptian temples of the neighbouring town, and these relics may have found a third use in the later mosques of the villages. Not at the site of Hanes and in its burial-ground alone must the old records be sought, but all around, if indeed Mariette's touching appeal be not disregarded. A French scholar of eminence is already in

Egypt, and has appealed to English sympathy to carry out researches which are of European interest. Great as is the importance of the one site here noticed, there are many others to which it must yield. Classical scholars must remember the old settlement of the trading Greeks at Naucratis, where the unearthing of the smallest fragment of pottery or glass would supply a link between the civilisations and the art of the northern and the southern coasts of the Mediterranean. Students of the Bible will not forget the land of Goshen, full of the hidden records of the Hebrew ages, Zoan the capital of Joseph's Pharaoh, the residence of the Pharaoh of the Exodus. To Goshen and to Zoan Mariette has markedly pointed in the scheme which he has bequeathed us, speaking with that foresight which seems to give a deep significance to the last words of one who has worked in earnest, and would tell us not what he has done, but what remains to be achieved. His best memorial will be the carrying through of this well-considered scheme. A noble work will then go on unchecked to due fulfilment.

CHAPTER IV.

THEBES.

No city of the old world can still show so much of her former splendour as Egyptian Thebes. Her ancient rival, Memphis, is marked alone by the vast necropolis, Babylon by shapeless ruins, Nineveh by buried palaces. Of imperial Rome not so much survives; luxurious Baghdad has dwindled to a poverty-stricken provincial town covering the ruins of the palaces of the masters of the East. Where are the sumptuous edifices of Constantine in his seat of empire? where the glittering domes of Teemoor at Samarkand? Elsewhere the imagination alone can revive the former glories of which the trace has been swept away, or over which the monuments of later time have cast new and transforming associations. At Thebes alone can you live again in the midst of the greatness of three thousand years ago, undisturbed by the changes of the times between and by the new life of to-day.

Not one of the many temples of Thebes has wholly disappeared; some are almost complete; many of the royal and private tombs were, until the tourist came, fresh with colours as of yesterday. Thebes yet stands, in spite of the centuries of trouble that presaged the Assyrian conquest, the ruthless sack by Assur-ban-habal, true grandson of Sennacherib, the raging wantonness of mad Cambyses, the iconoclastic zeal of the early Church, the barbarism of the stupid, utilitarian Turk. The beauty of the ancient city has even survived a worse enemy than all these, the selfish and vain modern tourist, who destroys a document of the world's history, or a record of antique belief, to carry away a few hieroglyphics he cannot understand, and, like a noxious reptile, marks his trail with the vulgar scrawl of his unknown name, while his asses are stalled in a royal tomb near by. One could fill pages with the story of this worst plague, telling how one tourist ordered her dragoman to cut out Joseph's head, as she thought it, from the only picture of the arrival of a Shemite family in Egypt; how others broke in by night and demolished a sculptured wall, to steal the single known figure portraying the wife of a chief of the land of spices; both priceless documents of history and ethnology. Besides the rage of conquerors and the industrious destruction of our ignorant fellow-countrymen, for they are the worst offenders, nature at Thebes is proving that even the massive architecture of Egypt cannot resist her patient forces. The nitrous soil is slowly undermining the vast columns of El-Karnak, which will some day fall in confused ruin as by the shock of an earthquake. But this final catastrophe of the greatest temple has not yet come. There, as elsewhere, we can still, in quiet chambers untouched by the army of spoilers, see the former magnificence of the capital; or, yet more, can be carried back into the past, when we descend into some little-visited royal tomb deep in the rock of the silent valley of the west, on whose walls yet shine the mystic pictures that portray the fate of the soul in the world beyond the grave.

The origin of the great city is obscure. Unlike Memphis, Thebes, her southern rival, rose to the headship by slow degrees. It was towards the close of the dark age marked by the rule of Hanes, that a new line of kings arose in the upper country, with Thebes for their capital. At first they were merely nobles; then one became a local king, and his successors won the whole dominion of Egypt. These were the sovereigns of the Eleventh Dynasty. Their date must be before Abraham, probably some centuries earlier; but it is not yet certain, so obscure is the early chronology of Egypt.

Thus it was not by deliberate selection, as in the wise choice of the site of Memphis by Menes, but by the accident of success, that a small provincial town became the capital of Egypt. The position was fit for a great city, but too far south for the centre of government, and nearer to the safe border of Ethiopia than to the assailable frontiers on the north-east and north-west.

More than four hundred miles, by the river, south of Cairo and Memphis, the Nile valley widens on the east, forming a great amphitheatre, bounded by the distant mountains; while on the west the same rocky barrier, after almost touching the river, retires, leaving a narrower semicircle. Unlike the level desert-wall of the rest of Egypt, the western mountain rises in a peak-like form to the unusual height of twelve hundred feet, and in one place falls to the plain in a sheer scarped cliff. The view from either side of the river is marked by features unusual in the country. We rarely see there so wide a plain encircled by mountains, though there are far ampler expanses with a rocky wall in the dim distance, and we never see pointed heights closing in the view. No monument stands on the river's bank save the temple of El-Uksur (Luxor), conspicuous with its long ranges of columns. In the distance we discern other great temples, the fortress-like gateway of El-Karnak, the ruined Rameseum, the massive pile of Medeenet-Haboo, and below the cliff the western hills, honeycombed with the entrances of tombs. The size of the monuments grows on us when we are near enough to gain a scale by which to measure them from some passing figure, but they lack the assertion of magnitude which the Pyramids, when first seen, owe more to their surroundings than to their dimensions. If the setting of Thebes is less advantageous than that of Memphis to the works of man, it is far more picturesque and beautiful. It has at once charms of form and of well-defined expanse, both exceptions to the rules of the Egyptian landscape; nor does it lack the great river, here broadened by islands, and offering long reaches of rushing water, the richly-coloured landscape, and the solemn desert-background of rock, all shining beneath a sky of far deeper blue than northern Egypt knows. Thus as at Memphis the Pyramids grow upon us, at Thebes it is the beauty of the scene; and we do not wonder that the old Egyptians, in the days of imperial power, preferred their own city to any other, better fitted, indeed, for the control of the country, but far less for repose, and that they loved to dwell in this beautiful circle, where the mountains seem to shut one in from the world around as in a quiet oasis.

Thebes, like the other cities of Egypt, had a civil and a religious name. The civil name was Apiu, 'the city of thrones,' which, with the article 't' or 'ta,' became Ta-Apiu, and was identified by the Greeks with the name of their own famous city, by us corruptly called Thebes. The sacred name was Nu-Amen, 'the city of Amen,' the god of Thebes; or simply Nu, 'the city,' and Nu-ā, 'the great city.'[1] In these names we recognise the No-Amon and No of Scripture.

The religion of Thebes was centred round the worship of Amen, 'the hidden,' in the form Amen-ra, which connected this local divinity with Ra, the sun, reverenced throughout Egypt. Thus when Thebes became the

[1] See Dümichen in Oncken's *Allgemeine Geschichte*, i. 77, 68.

capital of Egypt, Amen-ra was sometimes placed at the head of the Pantheon. He became both a solar divinity and the king of the gods. During the Empire, when the Theban line was supreme, it was to him that the kings prayed, to his temple that they brought the spoils of many wars and the tributes of many nations. It may be that at this time Amen became the god of the oases, and the famous oracle had its origin which carried his fame and worship, under the name of Ammon, to Greece herself, long before Alexander made his pilgrimage to the Oasis of Jupiter Ammon, and was saluted by the priest as the son of the divinity of the temple.

Such was the site and such the religion of Thebes. Her history cannot be told here, for it is the history of Egypt, almost the political history of the ancient world, for centuries. Yet the rise, the bloom, and the decay of the great city must be sketched. The first line that ruled there was succeeded by the Twelfth Dynasty, which lasted a little over two centuries, the happiest age of Egyptian history. The wise practical rulers of that time devoted their energy and their revenues to developing the vast agricultural wealth of the country: they watched the rising of the Nile and marked its annual level far up in Ethiopia; and one of them constructed a great artificial reservoir, the Lake Mœris, to drain off the superfluous waters and store them for use in irrigating the rich oasis in Middle Egypt, opening from the Nile valley, now called the Feiyoom. The country was then prosperous, and the rulers had no ambition of foreign dominion. The weaker Theban kings who followed this active line, or the yet obscurer rulers of Xoïs, were at last forced to submit to foreign overlords, the Shepherd-kings, whose story belongs to the city of Zoan. Centuries, how many or how few we know not, passed, and at last from Thebes arose the cry for independence. A Theban tributary of the stranger-king threw off the yoke, and led the nation in a long and terrible war, which only closed when Egypt was again free, and a king of Thebes once more the ruler of an undivided state. This was about B.C. 1600, when the Eighteenth Dynasty began.

The old capital was not abandoned. Perhaps a sentiment clung to the memory of her former greatness; perhaps the new kings desired to touch the loyalty of their own people, and to avoid the risk of moving the seat of dominion; perhaps they loved the restful beauty in which Thebes was set, to which she owed the long favour of her rulers. Thus the kings of the Eighteenth, Nineteenth, and Twentieth Dynasties, or we might say of the Egyptian Empire, which nearly equalled the duration of those royal lines, had Thebes for their capital. Temples and tombs alike bear witness to the splendour of this age, not the happiest, but the most brilliant, in the history of Egypt.

Then came the decline. Incessant wars abroad, discontent at home, and the rule of feeble kings, worked the fall of the Empire; and the great city was no longer the constant seat of government, though whoso held it added to the adornment of its temples on the lesser scale of the ever-waning power. Yet even in Homer's time, when the hand of decay had been heavy for some three centuries, Thebes was the greatest city within the poet's horizon, both for her store of wealth and for her mighty chariot-force which was then the backbone of war. And about two centuries later the prophet Nahum wrote a vivid description of Thebes and of her resources. In this passage, where the name No-Amon alone occurs in Scripture, the prophet warns Nineveh by the fate of a rival not inferior to herself, and but lately sacked by the Assyrian king. He says, 'Art thou better than No-Amon, that was enthroned ("the city of thrones") among the Nile-streams, the waters round about her, whose rampart [was] the sea (the Nile), her wall of the sea. Cush and Mizraim [were] her strength, and [it was] infinite, Put and Lubim were thy helpers' (Nahum iii. 8, 9). Then follows the piteous narrative of the sack, the merciless slaughter, and the sale and captivity of even the great men among the inhabitants (ver. 10). Assurban-habal gives us the same story in the true Assyrian regal style. He tells how Thebes was treated as a conquered town, despoiled of gold and silver, of precious stones and costly stuffs, of horses; of the treasure of the palace, of a booty which could not be counted, of men and women, of works of the sculptor, all of which were carried to Nineveh. This was in about B.C. 666 or 665. Before the century had closed, the same fate befel Nineveh herself.

From this great blow Thebes never recovered: succeeding kings endeavoured to repair her shattered edifices, but Cambyses, the Persian conqueror, repeated the vengeance of the Assyrian, and despite the care of the earlier Greek kings, Thebes had the misfortune to be twice the centre of revolt against the Ptolemies. At the close of the reign of Philopator, an independent dynasty was established, which was overthrown by Epiphanes. The Thebans rose once more against Lathyrus. The patriotic party made their last stand in the old city, which endured a three years' siege, but was at length taken and dealt with by the successful king according to his ruthless temper. This was the end of the City of Thrones, since represented only by scattered villages about the temples.

The final decline of Thebes before the fall of paganism, and the distance of any later rival, have saved the monuments from being used, like those of Memphis, for the building materials of successive capitals. Thus in the early part of this century the aspect of the site must have been little changed from that which it presented when Ptolemy Lathyrus drew off his vindictive forces. The industry in detail of the ignorant tourist, who labours like the rat and the worm, has worked more mischief than any force of nature; and fifty years of systematic spoliation has been more injurious than the swift rage of conquerors. Yet nearly all the great edifices yet stand, and the sequence of pictures in the royal tombs can still be followed.

Of all the temples of Egypt, if not of the whole world, the chief edifice of Thebes, now called the temple of El-Karnak, on the eastern side, is probably the greatest, certainly the most costly. It was dedicated to Amen-ra, and was the central shrine of Egypt throughout the days of the Empire. A patient German scholar, Dr. Dümichen, has published a beautiful plan of the whole structure with its surrounding lesser temples, printing in different colours the successive additions; from which it appears that from the Twelfth Dynasty to the Greek kings, during more than two thousand years, we may discriminate the works of twenty-four periods, six denoting royal lines, eighteen representing single reigns which were chiefly remarkable for large additions.[1]

No great cathedral or abbey shows such a vast succession of labour nor so continuous a history. It is not alone that we have here the styles of many ages, and the tastes of monarchs of different origin, but every part of the vast accumulation is inscribed within and without with religious representations and historical scenes, with the stiff pictures of acts of homage to the gods, and the lively portrayals of great victories, all with explanatory

[1] See Dr. Dümichen's History already referred to.

inscriptions. It is not alone a temple, but a library of historical records. Here is the long list of the conquests of Shishak, which mentions the Levite cities of Israel and the strongholds of Judah; here the still earlier treaty of Ramses II. with the Hittites, that long-forgotten power, now only emerging from oblivion, which of old successfully divided with Egypt the Empire of the East. These are but items in the list of precious documents which cover the walls of the temple. Yet more remains below the earth, for every clearing of the chambers yields new treasures.

This temple, all built of solid stone, is from its stupendous size among temples what the Great Pyramid is among tombs. The width of the great entrance-gateway facing the west is over 360 feet. The first court measures 329 feet broad by 275 feet long, and thence we pass into the hall of assembly, supported by 134 columns, those of the central avenue being near 70 feet high and about 12 feet in diameter, those of the side avenues over 40 feet high and about 9 feet in diameter. The great columns have capitals in the cup-like form of the papyrus, the lesser ones capitals in the shape of the lotus bud. In this vast hall the cathedral of Notre Dame could stand without touching the walls. Though marked by the calamities of Thebes, this wondrous monument of her greatness is still overpoweringly grand; a forest of columns rises on every side, and we can scarcely believe we move amidst the work of men of our strength and our measure. Going farther, we note the two standing obelisks of red granite, one the work of an ambitious woman, Queen Hatasu, a single block, 108 feet high, the tallest in the world, formerly coated with fine gold, at once a historic monument, an architectural adornment, and a lightning-conductor.[1] The inscription on its pedestal tells us that the whole labour of quarrying, engraving, and setting up this great monolith took only nineteen months. Here and beyond, the remains of the temple are heaped up in confusion that makes us wonder at the patience which could have destroyed no less than at the patience which first constructed the mighty mass, once in stately order, now piled up in mountainous heaps.

Another great temple, that of El-Uksur, is on the same bank of the river; but we must cross to the

[1] The Egyptian obelisks had a threefold purpose. Standing before the temple-gates, they bore dedicatory inscriptions, and cut the long horizontal lines against which they were relieved, while capped and coated with gold, they served as lightning-conductors.

western side, the side of the tombs, and note the succession of sepulchral temples. In yet older times, each pyramid had its chapel, not within the building, as in private tombs, but in front, for the greater security of the royal sepulchre, which was finally closed when the king's great sarcophagus was slid down to its resting-place. Similarly the Theban kings of the Empire were buried in a secluded valley, behind the mountain, that seems to guard their tombs as it rises to unwonted height, and falls in a sharp precipice in front of the royal burial-ground. Along the edge of the desert, beneath the mountain, rises a series of temples, which, though dedicated to gods, yet were the sepulchral chapels of the kings, telling to future time the achievements of their reigns, while the story of their fate in what the Egyptians called 'the other world' was reserved for the walls of their mysterious tombs. Beginning at the north, we first see the temple which Ramses II. completed for his father and grandfather. Then we reach the greater monument he built for his own renown, the Rameseum. Here, in the first court, lies a fallen Colossus of the king, in red granite, once 60 feet in height, and weighing over 887 tons, one solid mass, the greatest monolithic statue in Egypt or in the world, yet hurled down and broken by the Assyrian or the Persian. This temple, for purity of curve and line in its columns, and for the liveliness of its war-scenes, is nowhere excelled among Egyptian monuments. The two Statues in the Plain, only second in size to the fallen one of Ramses, are almost all that remain of the great temple of Amenoph III., an earlier sovereign. Yet farther is the vast pile of Medeenet Haboo, the temple of Ramses III., on the walls of which we see the story of his wars with the maritime nations of the Mediterranean, like a Homeric poem in sculpture, and among them we take note of the oldest portrayal of a naval battle, in which the Egyptian galleys win the victory against the sea-folk of the Mediterranean. Besides these, close under the cliff, is the temple of Queen Hatasu and her brothers, Thothmes II. and III., of which the chief interest lies in the tale told both in pictures and words of the expedition the adventurous queen sent to the land of spices, bringing away its costly products, of which the balm-bearing trees were planted in the capital. Of the third Thothmes, the greatest Egyptian conqueror, the records are more interesting at El-Karnak than here.

Between the temples and the mountain, either in detached hills or in the plain, are the seemingly countless tombs of the Theban people, full, so far as the tourist has spared them, of those marvellous pictures which enable us to transport ourselves back to the everyday life of three thousand years ago, yet all telling of the other world, the preparations for the last rites, the funeral procession, the life to come. In the delicate inscriptions, of which every letter or word is a painted hieroglyphic, now ruthlessly mutilated, were repeated the lament of the wailing women, the cry of the bereaved wife, the dirge which at once saddened and cheered the funeral feast. For that strange assembly, with eating and drinking, music and dancing, while it paid the last honours to the dead, was counselled in the plaintive song of the harper to enjoy life, not unmindful of its duties and of its end. Some idea of the splendour of these monuments may be gained from the fact that the largest tomb has an area in its excavations of over 23,000 square feet, and occupies nearly an acre and a quarter of rock, all the walls of the series of chambers except those of sepulture being sculptured; but this is a giant among the Theban sepulchres.

Far behind, in the hidden valley, are the tombs of the kings of the Empire, deeply cut into the rock, and covered with the mystic paintings and inscriptions which record the Egyptian belief as to the world to come, with its trials, its rewards, and its punishments, all defaced by the modern spoiler, though forty years ago some were almost untouched. The royal tombs are vacant, but the last discovery at Thebes has brought some of their most famous tenants to the upper air. On this side the valley under the western cliff, a great sepulchral hiding-place was found, whither more than thirty mummies, mostly regal, had been taken for safety in ancient times. Thus Thothmes III., the great conqueror, and Ramses II., the great oppressor, are once more seen in the light of day. If the Museum of Boolák has escaped the fanatical and greedy mob of Cairo, we may there in the presence of her ancient kings feel, as at Thebes, how Egypt obliterates time and brings the present and past together as by magic art.

Such is the briefest catalogue of the wonders of Egyptian Thebes, that great and ancient city, which of all the capitals of the world speaks most eloquently of the times that are past, and echoes the thoughts of forgotten ages, telling the story of the vicissitudes of earthly fortune as a warning, uttering the cry of human hope and fear for the hereafter as an encouragement.

CHAPTER V.

ZOAN.

As we look at a country and try to connect the forms of nature and the homes of men with the events of history, we find that by degrees our eyes are attracted to the points of special interest. These are usually the central stronghold, sometimes one town, sometimes another, always in the heart of the land, and the border that could easily be assailed. The one has a history telling how the nation grew, the other has lays recording how it resisted the invader. The border has the more stirring annals, falling of their own accord into the shape of verse, save at those moments when this first line of defence has been overleapt and the struggle for existence fought under the ramparts of the capital, themselves now the border of the land. Thus Paris, in the Norman sieges, became far more interesting than Chalons or Roncesvalles ; the Monastery of the Troitza, in the great Polish war, than the shifting eastern limits of Russia, where the Tartars were repulsed. In English history the border is everything. What is Winchester, or even Windsor or Westminster, beside Alnwick or Naworth? Verse is silent as to the royal seats, save in the poem of the captive Scottish king; but for centuries sings the story of the changeful wars and forays of the marches.

Egypt is no exception to the common rule. Secure on the south and rarely assailed on the west, she was ever open to attack on the east. True the desert where Sabaco lost his way, as he fled alone from the rout of Raphia, and only escaped by the friendly aid of a Philistine shepherd; and the treacherous footing of the Serbonian bog, 'where armies whole have sunk,' were a barrier against the invader. Yet an Arab tribe, bought by money or attracted by the greed for plunder, could lead him through the pathless waste, and the great plain of Lower Egypt once in sight, he need not even bridge the Nile, he had only to follow the right bank of the eastern branch as far as Heliopolis, and then Memphis on the other side of the single stream could be assailed at leisure, when he had boats for the passage. Thus while the centres of national life, Memphis and Thebes, attract us, the border-land has a more potent charm. There stood, from the days before Abraham, the fortresses, carefully constructed on principles we are pleased in our ignorance to call modern, with scarp and counterscarp, and ditch and glacis, well manned by the best troops, the sentinel on the ramparts day and night; there were fought the decisive battles, twice at Raphia beyond the border, once at Pelusium within; how many more times we know not, for native history, eloquent of success through long ages, is silent of disaster, which is told only by the allusions of foreign annals.

The border population of all lands is the strongest. None but vigorous races could live in the din of war, varied by the dreadful calm that presages invasion. Either the stoutest of the people were set in the front rank by royal purpose or their own daring choice, or strangers were chosen for a post which the natives were not hardy enough to hold. Thus our own borderers, from whom the Highland regiments are largely recruited, are not alone partly of the finest Saxon stock, whether they call themselves English or Scottish, but there flows in their veins the blood of the Roman cohorts, Spaniards, Gauls, Moors, Thracians, Dalmatians, and others, who defended the Wall against the barbarians in the utmost limits of the Empire as stoutly as those who in after time followed the banners of the Howards and the Percies against the Scots.

In Egypt, whether by settled design of the Pharaohs, or by emigration and conquest, the disputed border fell to the share of Shemite settlers; and from Abraham's time to our own, a brave people, larger in bone, and stronger in muscle, and of broader shoulders than the Egyptians, and of a more independent temper, has pastured its herds in the vast luxuriant plain, and fished the prolific waters of the great eastern lake.

It is hard to define a border-land. We know how with ourselves it shifted with the two Roman Walls, and the changing overlordship of Northumberland. Yet it may always be roughly sketched out, allowing for its narrowness in times of peace, and its extension in the strife of war, by the pressure of a conqueror from without, or of a strong government from within. But the Egyptian border never varied on its outer side : we have only to determine its depth. Nature had drawn the boundary-line on the east with final precision. Egypt, whether ruled by native or by stranger, could never extend beyond the limits of the great plain. No enemy could establish himself within these limits unless he conquered the whole Delta, for the broad desert was left behind him. In prosperous times, the Pharaohs affected to rule the waste of sand; but all that they controlled was a chain of castles which commanded the great road. They could no more make the barren desert a part of fruitful Egypt, than they could catch and tame the wild Arabs who there roamed at their will. But while the eastern limit was thus fixed, it is hard to say how far the borderland, with its peculiar population, stretched to the west and to the south. If we are guided by the names of towns, which are either Shemite, or both Shemite and Egyptian, by local worship, and by the peculiarities of race, we may put the Tanitic branch of the Nile as the general western limit, continuing the border along the edge of Lake Menzeleh to its farther extremity, and may take the old canal of the Red Sea as the southern boundary. This is but a fragment of Lower Egypt, but it is 'the best of the land;' once wealthy in towns, each a treasure-house of history, in part already told, but far more lying beneath the earth awaiting the tardy explorer. In the centre is the land of Goshen, southward of the field of Zoan. The city of Zoan, the civil capital of Joseph's Pharaoh, the residence of the Pharaoh of the Exodus, stood near the western limit. The great stronghold of Pelusium, or Sin, marked the north-eastern point; not far to the south stood the scarcely inferior Migdol, the frontier fortress in Ezekiel's time; a neighbouring mound, some one of these sepulchres of forgotten greatness, must entomb the military settlement of Avaris, which commanded the border, when it was at once the place of arms and the last possession of the mysterious Shepherds who are soon to come into the field of our view.

Of the towns which crowded this strip of land, by far the most important was Zoan, or Tanis. This was natural. The border bristled with fortresses in the old days of the Pharaohs; but in their rear, away from the shock of war, must have lain a great city, far behind the first river, as Pelusium stood before it. This city must have been on the eastern bank of the second stream, to hold the passage if the first line of defence should be forced, and to be a rallying-point if that line should be turned.

An isolated passage in the Bible, breaking like a note

the narrative of the journey of the Spies, follows the mention of Hebron, and the mighty Anakim who ruled there: 'Now Hebron was built seven years before Zoan in Egypt' (Numb. xiii. 22). What a glimpse of all we have lost is here, like the epitaph of the forgotten nations in Balaam's prophecy. Once it was well known when both these ancient cities were built, and now we can but grope in the darkness. Perhaps it was written in one of the lost books, the Book of Jasher or the Book of the Wars of the Lord, lost as hopelessly as most of the contents of the Alexandrian library, yet current in a literary age, when there was a city of books (Kirjath Sepher) in Canaan, and when the Hittite king who reigned in Syria before the Exodus, took his 'writer of books' to battle with him.

Leaving speculation, we must look to the scanty records, few, but precious in information, which the genius of Mariette first read in the ruins of Zoan. The city was already standing in the remote days of the Sixth Dynasty, the last powerful line of Memphis, and flourishing under the prosperous Theban Twelfth Dynasty, in the time of Abraham, if not much earlier. The position, excellent, as we have seen, for the protection of the border, had also every commercial advantage. A great seat of land traffic should stand as near as possible to the eastern border; it should have a harbour secure from war and storms, and conveniently situate to shelter the galleys of the rich Phœnician marts. Such an emporium should be on the great water-way, so that the loads of the camels of Midianite and Canaanite merchants, and the cargoes of the ships of Tarshish, might be at once carried on to Memphis and to Thebes. Such was Zoan, wisely chosen to be the Alexandria of primitive Egypt.

Zoan must have shared the general decline that followed the bright days of the Twelfth Dynasty, and have been almost the first town to fall under the rule of a conquering race, who appear after a time of darkness as the rulers of Egypt. These were the Shepherds, or Hyksos, as to whom almost all our true information has been found by Mariette in the mounds of the forgotten city. When they invaded the country, how they conquered it, how long they ruled it, we do not know. All we can say is that towards the close of their dominion they raised the monuments we see at Zoan, the great works of Apepi, who reigned about seventeen centuries before our Era, and seems to have been the Pharaoh of Joseph. The strong military station of Avaris, probably farther to the east, is spoken of as the royal residence at this time. The sculptures of the Shepherds show, however, the importance at that day of Zoan, which is thought, with reason, to have been the civil capital.

We must pause at the mention of Joseph's Pharaoh, and remember that the whole period of the Hebrew sojourn is closely interwoven with the history of Zoan. Here ruled the king in whose name Egypt was governed by the Hebrew, who was no less than regent; here ruled those who still favoured the people of Israel. Under the great Oppression, Zoan was a royal residence. Zoan was the starting-point of the great journey of the deliverance. Would that those who care for Bible history would search here for the Egyptian annals of those days!

In the reign of Apepi, the Theban kings, possibly discontented with Joseph's strong rule, began to make head against their foreign overlords. A mighty struggle ensued; and at length the strangers were forced back on Asia. Avaris was stormed, and Zoan once more fell into the hands of the Egyptians. The Shepherds departed, rulers and fighting men, as many as survived the long war; but the common folk remained, and Zoan and the country round became a foreign city and land to the Egyptians.

The Hebrews thus changed masters, and from subjects of the Shepherds, became slaves of the Egyptians. They had been invited to settle by a Shepherd king, either Apepi or another like him, who, though he took the style of the Pharaohs, had his sympathies in the East, and would people his new country with races, if not akin to his own, yet nearer to it than the Egyptians in their ways of life. The Hebrews were welcomed as settlers, and planted in the fertile land of Goshen. Suddenly, instead of favoured subjects, they became part of a body of serfs, hated and dreaded by their masters; for to the Shepherd name clung the memory of past rule, embittered by the sense of oppression, and awaking the fear that the olden condition might come back with a single change of fickle fortune. So began the great Hebrew servitude.

Aahmes, the king who conquered and expelled the strangers, was head of the Eighteenth Dynasty, which began about B.C. 1600. That family ruled during the first period of the Egyptian Empire, a time of two centuries. The sympathies of the new rulers were with Ethiopia. No doubt it was by aid from the south that the mastery of Egypt was won: there are indications which may point to an Ethiopian alliance. As the conquering kings, with all the energy of the leaders of a race newly awakened to discover its strength, passed eastwards, and speedily subdued an Empire which had Assyria as the farthest province, the subject race of Egypt could expect no favour. That race was but part of the mass of the conquered, the prey of the new force that impelled the Pharaohs, in expedition after expedition, across the eastern border.

All this time history is silent as to Zoan and the lands around. They were neglected and oppressed. No doubt the frontier fortresses were strongly held; but much of the old commercial wealth found other channels. Partly it followed the route of the Red Sea, and crossed the desert of the Thebaïs; partly it may have been diverted to the Phœnician towns, and passed by land along the military roads, leaving Zoan, and following the border of the cultivated country towards Memphis.

It is most remarkable that this same period is equally a blank in the sacred history. For above two centuries, from the death of Joseph to the birth of Aaron, or from the end of the time of prosperity to the beginning of the heaviest oppression, we have scarcely any hint of the state of the Hebrews. Here again is a cogent reason for exploration of sites in this district.

The Eighteenth Dynasty decayed and ended in the confusion of a religious conflict. A new family, the Nineteenth, the line of the kings nearly all of whom bore the name of Ramses, the Ramessides, gained the throne, and the second age of the Empire began; another two centuries of less extensive conquest but of more organised rule abroad, and at home yet more fertile in memorials of the time. It seems that these kings were akin to the old rulers of Zoan, the Hyksos. Whether this be so or not, the eastern border now became a favourite part of Egypt. New cities, both frontier strongholds and centres of trade, arose everywhere. Zoan was rebuilt, and called Pe-Ramses, 'the house of Ramses,' carefully distinguished in the inscriptions as Ramses II., first apparently the name of a quarter, then that of the whole city. The name thus marks the new founder as Ramses II., the great oppressor of the Israelites, who 'built for Pharaoh treasure-cities' (or store-cities), 'Pithom and Raamses'

(Exod. i. 11), the latter called elsewhere, as in the route of the Exodus, Rameses. This was when the great heat of the Oppression began.

How was it that a king, who seems to have had the blood of the serf population in his veins, and who specially favoured their part of Egypt, was at the same time the great oppressor of the Hebrew section of the people? The Shepherds had been long subdued; but, by a subtle influence, they had conquered their conquerors with the arms wherewith the Greeks led the Romans captive. The age of the Ramessides is marked by a new literary life. Hitherto the Egyptians had written much on papyrus-paper and the pictured walls of the temples and the tombs; they had written for the sake of religion and duty, with patient method and studious care. Now they write for writing's sake, not alone in the old manner, but on every material, on the very potsherds that still strew the ruins of their ancient towns. The old literature, like a mummy come to life again, bursts the bonds of priestly rule, and sings new verse with native freedom. An epic poem and beautiful hymns are of this age. Of the same time are a multitude of letters, now in European museums, mostly written in the very town of Rameses.

This fresh literature is steeped with Shemite, or, if you will, Hebrew, influence. When he knows a Hebrew word, the scribe prefers to use it for the corresponding one in the Egyptian. Words are but the vehicles of ideas; but they change the thoughts which they convey. Here, however, their work is but insignificant; the ideas were already changed before they found a new expression. This is a fresh outburst of feeling, the source of a young and vigorous literary life.

Some may hesitate to believe that the Egyptians, nourished by centuries of culture, had aught to learn from wandering shepherds or serfs, who scarcely held even their lives secure. But these are shallow doubts, common enough to modern dwellers in great cities, surrounded by the neglected wealth of ancient literatures. Let them ask whether either Homer, or the writers of the Sagas, or Llywarch Hên and Taliesin, or the ancient Irish poets, or the Arabs before Mohammad, or the unknown authors of the earlier Spanish ballads, lived as we do. Were they not all wanderers? Did most of them even write? The old Arabs were one of the most literary nations in the world, whose warrior-poets contended for the prize of verse alone in their native

Olympic meeting; yet they dwelt in tents, and rarely wrote their complicated odes. Such were the ancient dwellers in Lower Egypt. How many poets may have sung before Moses we know not; but the Egyptians heard the songs of their captivity, and learnt melodies unknown before.

So there grew a bond between the two races. The Egyptians, unlike their rulers, showed kindness to the Hebrews, and were remembered kindly for this in after times. The races mixed. The Hebrews bore Egyptian names. When we find a Moses (Messu), or a Phinehas (Pi-nahsi), in the inscriptions, we need not think him an Israelite. The Egyptians took Hebrew names, and if Rui, the name of the high-priest of Thebes, is the same as Levi, we need not infer that he is not an Egyptian.

In all this Ramses saw a danger. The state was fast becoming oriental. What if the old masters should win again what they had lost? He could not stop the tide of Egyptian thought, but he could separate and crush the foreign element which had set it in action. Hence the great persecution, during which the city Rameses, built by serf-labour, rose to magnificence Zoan had never known.

It was at this time that the city recovered her old political and commercial consequence. Here Ramses and his son Menptah, the Pharaoh of the Exodus, held their court whenever any expedition was preparing. Hence the presence of the Pharaohs during the Oppression, hence the 'wonders in the field of Zoan,' for so the southern part of the nome or province was called.

These memorable events belong more fitly to the story of the town and land of Goshen, the next subject. We must here follow the fortunes of Zoan, which waned with the decline of the Empire, and rose again when a Tanite Dynasty, the Twenty-first, ruled Egypt, not without the resistance of rival lines. This family has an interest in history, from the alliance by treaty and marriage with Solomon. A later Dynasty, the Twenty-third, seems also to have reigned here; and Zoan was still important in Isaiah's age, but henceforward her decline was certain. Pelusium first, and Alexandria later, usurped her place; and now a miserable village retains her name, and gives emphasis to the evidence of the lofty mounds and demolished temples, as, startled by the melancholy solitude around us, we remember the glowing lines in which an old Egyptian poet, whom we shall later quote, depicts the beauty which was the setting of the city he calls incomparable even with Thebes..

History has much to say of Zoan ; the site can as yet tell us little : what we gather there is rather general than local. The temples are fallen, and their very fragments shattered ; the tombs are still undiscovered. It will be hard to gain any knowledge of the city on the spot, until some one shall have taken the pains to dig into the vast mounds which cover a store-house of historic treasure, almost certainly containing contemporary records of the sojourn, the oppression, and the Exodus of the Hebrews. The book is there ; who will reach down his hand for it and open and read its ancient pages? Yet from the fragments which lie on the very surface, or have been found just beneath it, an outline may be sketched, and other sources will help to tint a canvas, which must remain blank in its details, like a picture true in colouring, but so vague in form that it should only be looked at from a distance.

The name of Zoan is mysterious. The modern Sán preserves, like its Greek, Latin, and Coptic equivalents, the same word as the Hebrew Zoan ; and Zoan again is found in the Egyptian Za'n or Za' in the phrase which exactly represents the Hebrew 'field of Zoan.' Thus we have an uninterrupted pedigree to the time of Moses. Yet the old Egyptian name of the city, as given in the hieroglyphic inscriptions, is not Za'n, but Zal (Zar) or Zalu. Both Za'n and Zal are not Egyptian, but foreign words; and we cannot consider them to be ordinary varieties of dialect. It may be that they existed side by side, that Zal was the classical, and Za'n the popular, form, but this is mere conjecture. Pe-Ramses, shortened by the Hebrews to Raamses, or Rameses, presents no difficulty. The name is historically important as a link in the chain of evidence for the date of the Exodus. The building of Rameses, as already shown, marks the founder Ramses II. as the great oppressor of the Hebrews. Consequently his son and successor Menptah must have been the Pharaoh of the Exodus.[1]

The worship of Zoan cannot be satisfactorily known until the site has been thoroughly explored. It seems, however, that the first divinity was Ptah, the creator, the god of Memphis. This was during the rule of the Memphites and the old Thebans. The Shepherds set up the worship of Sutech, a form of Set or Typhon, reverenced

[1] The geographical identifications are adopted from Dr. Brugsch.

G

in Egypt as physical evil, the embodiment of the desert, and the sea, darkness, and the storm, the opponent of Osiris, the good being, the Nile, and light. He was also specially the patron of foreigners, the power who swept the children of the desert like a sandstorm over the fertile land. Sutech thus succeeded Ptah, and held this place throughout the Empire. With the Empire, however, the worship of the sun-gods was introduced; and when at length Sutech or Set was expelled from the Pantheon, through a confusion of moral with physical evil, the chief divinity became Horus, the sun of the day. There are thus three periods of the religion of Zoan, corresponding to the three foundations of the city, those of the Memphite, the Shepherd, and the mixed Theban worship, and a fourth period due to an innovation. It must not be thought, however, that ever, save for a time under the Shepherds, there was one system to the exclusion of the rest. At all other ages the general belief of the whole country admitted the joint reverence of several divinities. Thus while Ramses II. maintained the foreign religion, he also preserved the still earlier worship, and added to it the popular reverence for the sun-gods, whom as the child of the sun, for so we understand his name, he specially reverenced.

We have a picture of Zoan in the days of Ramses, in the words of an Egyptian poet, which lights up its sombre aspect of to-day with the vivid colours of three thousand years ago; as when one passes from the barren, deathly, sun-smitten desert into the refreshing cool of a newly opened sepulchral chapel, lively with the harmonious brightness in which the old nation rejoiced.

'I arrived at the city of Ramses-mi-amen.' 'She is' 'beautiful, beautiful. There is nought like her among the monuments of Thebes,' 'the very secret of the pleasures of life. Her fields are full of lovely places, abounding in the produce of food daily, her pools are full of fish, her ponds of ducks, her meadows are verdant with herbage, the bower with blooming garlands. The garden is perfumed with the odour of honey; the meadow-land is steeped in moisture. Her granaries are full of wheat and barley, heaped up as high as heaven, vegetables and reeds (are) in the garden of herbs; flowers for posies in the fruit-house; lemons, citrons of two kinds, figs, in the orchard; sweet wine' there is 'which one mixes with honey;' fish of various kinds, some from the Euphrates, others such as are presented to the greatest of conquerors. 'The pond of Har-phra (is there), containing salt, the well containing natron. Her (ships) go and come daily, laden with products for food. The joys have there fixed their seat, there is no word of want; the small are there as the great.' Then follows the invitation to keep the festival of the fourth month. We see the joyous people bearing 'branches, posies from the orchard, garlands from the garden, the fowler with his thousands of birds.' The sea brings the king her tribute of fish, the distant lands their tributes. The people bear on their heads fresh skins of sweet drink. They stand at their doors, waving posies, branches, and garlands, for the king is making his entry in the morning.[1] This was not in spring-time, but in our ' chill October,' when Egypt is awakened by the cool north breeze, and refreshed with the waters of the wide-spread inundation. Such was 'the best of the land,' 'the land of Rameses' (Gen. xlvii. 11).

The vast monotonous plain of the Delta is broken when we see on the horizon the lofty mounds of Zoan. All around is desolation. When the Nile has spread over the land, marsh-plants spring up, and there are

[1] Chabas, *Mélanges Égyptologiques*, II. sér., p. 132, foll.

scanty patches of vegetation to point a contrast; but the dry season withers all, and then the whole tract is one brown space of desolate sameness. A few date-sellers may cross the mound, and that is all the commerce. Arabs of the western desert here chase the gazelle with falcon and greyhound. No description need emphasize these few words. There is indeed no scenery to describe; one vast silent solitude, without variety of form or colour, a weary wilderness; all the sadder when we think that the hard soil beneath our feet would yield a triple harvest, if war, neglect, and tyranny had not depopulated, and thus had marred, 'the best of the land.'

The ruins of Zoan are far too confused to admit of detailed description. We know their former magnificence, but we cannot restore their ancient shape. The sumptuous edifices lie in confused heaps, thrown down by man's violence or the force of an earthquake. There are also striking evidences of the agency of fire (*cf.* Ezek. xxx. 14). Two temples stood there, both wholly built of red granite of Syene, transported from the southern limit of Egypt, almost seven hundred miles away, monuments of a lavish expenditure, wonderful even in the days of Ramses, the rebuilder of the great temple, and the founder of the temple on the east. No less than fourteen obelisks adorned the great temple; and in this respect Zoan seems to have been far richer than any other Egyptian city, except perhaps Thebes and Heliopolis. The architecture must also have been peculiar in construction, for the proper place of the obelisks was in front of the entrance of a temple; and when, as at El-Karnak, we find more than a pair, this is due to the enlargement of the edifice in front of the old entrance. At Zoan these monoliths must have stood in the courts as well as in the approach. In cost of material and of work, the two temples are unsurpassed, as though Ramses had intended to astonish strangers with a splendid gateway at the entrance into Egypt. Not the Rameseum of Thebes, or the rock-cut temple of Aboo-Simbel in Nubia, wholly his work, nor even the hall of columns of El-Karnak, partly his, approach the magnificence of the great temple of Zoan. This must have been his favourite temple, at his chosen royal residence, and by it we can measure the ancient glory of Zoan.

The crude brick wall around, and the massive crude brick fort, must have been the result of such labours as those of the oppressed Hebrews; and as we look at them we think of the solitary leader who dared the successor of Ramses, and contrast the enduring spiritual work of Moses with the shattered material trophies of the great oppressor of his people.[1]

Once more I would enforce what I have said and written again and again, nor will yet cease to repeat, that here in Zoan and the country round is the place which we ought to explore that we may recover the lost Egyptian annals of the Hebrew sojourn. Our failure in this duty is a disgrace to our love of knowledge, a scandal to our love of the Bible. We have an evil eminence in Europe for our neglect of research in Egypt. It may be difficult to raise funds for work in Greece or Turkey, but there is no excuse for the polite indifference of the educated class to a subject which deeply interests the half-educated population, even to the children of the village schools. Would that some prophet should arise to make a worthy protest, and call on the

---

[1] Notices of Zoan will be found in the *Description de l'Égypte*, tom. v. pp. 99. foll. : Wilkinson's *Modern Egypt and Thebes*, i. 449, foll. : Mariette, *Notice des monuments* (Cat. Boolák Museum). Appendice : *Palestine Exploration Fund, Quarterly Statement*, July 1880, p. 133 ; Report by the Rev. Greville J. Chester. The next paper, which will be on the town and land of Goshen, will be illustrated by a map useful for this paper also.

Pharaoh of wasted opportunity and ill-spent wealth, to set free the priceless records his tyranny holds in bondage. The French have worked here and elsewhere in Egypt with well-rewarded vigour; why should not we give them our aid, and brighten the last years of our boasted nineteenth century with the glory of great discoveries, so that when we have ended our labours, our children may say, 'We can remember the excavations in the field of Zoan, and the land of Goshen'?

CHAPTER VI.

GOSHEN.

TRADITION is an unsafe guide, and never more so than in fixing the scenes of memorable events. Their interest fades and vanishes. Should it revive, it attaches itself to some new tale which wears the air of a recollection, though it is no more than a guess or a theory.

When travellers began to visit Egypt, they asked to be shown the land of Goshen, the ruins of the capital of the Pharaohs of the sojourn, the route of the Exodus, the place where the Israelites crossed the Red Sea. Nearly three thousand years, or ninety generations of men, had elapsed since the great event which began the national history of Israel. The Egyptians had become absorbed in the Arab race, and had forgotten their ancient learning. The travellers came with no better information than that of the commentators on the Bible, Hebrew and

Christian, to whom the names in the text were names and nothing more. They inquired of the natives of Egypt, and the answer was given from local tradition.

Standing on the western platform of the Citadel of Cairo, the visitor beheld, as he thought, the sites of sacred history spread out in the map of that splendid prospect, unsurpassed in the world for beauty and interest. Opposite were the pyramids of the great city of Memphis, the capital of Joseph's Pharaoh and of the oppressors; on the left, the mountains which hid the 'Valley of the Wandering' leading to the head of the Red Sea, pointed out as the place where the Hebrews crossed; and on the right, in far distance, the glittering green plain which spread north-eastwards to the land of Goshen, the utmost limits of which could even be seen. These mighty pyramids were the work of the enslaved Hebrews; from that pleasant land they moved towards the great capital, and waited for the signal of their freedom just below, perhaps where the many minarets and domes of Cairo now rise, until at length they passed safely behind the promontory, through the desert valley, towards the Red Sea, where, under the solemn mountains, the crowning deliverance was wrought. Nothing could be more dramatic than such a noble frame for those great events.

The Bible tells us nothing of Memphis at this time, nor of a southward journey. Whence, then, came the tradition? Not from the Bible, but from the Kurán. It was at Memphis that Mohammad placed the residence of the Pharaohs of the sojourn; and this central fact once believed by the Arabs as an article of faith, all the rest followed. When the Kurán was written, the official capital of Egypt was the fortress called Egyptian Babylon, close to the south of Cairo; and the renown of Memphis, on the opposite bank of the Nile, was as yet undimmed by time. Zoan had disappeared from memory. Whether Mohammad fixed an old local tradition, or framed a new one, little matters. Its persistence is clearly due to him.

We must turn reluctantly from this poetic vision, and, as though awaking from a pleasant dream to the hard work of life, face the severe critical inquiry which so great a problem demands, now that modern science has given us an array of facts. The result, in its truth, will charm us not less than the old fancy. It will certainly make our faith stronger in the venerable record which is part of the title-deeds of religion; for in place of the difficulties of the former identification, which would be hard to reconcile with a historical narrative, we find that beautiful agreement of place with circumstance which is the very test of true history.

The facts we need have been collected with admirable industry by Dr. Brugsch, who has devoted himself with indomitable patience to searching them out of the ancient Egyptian records of geography. The Egyptians were a scientific people, but they did not write dictionaries for our use. So the laborious scholar had to hunt up and down in lists of the temples relating to local worship, as well as in papyri recording royal donations, or giving in some form or other geographical information. He has published a series of volumes on the subject, the last of which is a great geographical dictionary, entirely written by lithography, for hieroglyphic type was too costly for him. In this work we have all necessary information that the old records have as yet yielded. For more we need excavations, the crying want of all who care for Bible history.

These new documents reveal this startling fact, that the land of Goshen had for very long been sufficiently defined on good authority. We possessed the information and never generally received it. So it lay almost useless for centuries.

The Septuagint, or Alexandrian Greek translation of the Old Testament, tells us what Dr. Brugsch has confirmed from the monuments. As we now possess this work, the dates of its various parts are different, representing a succession of labours; but it is clear that the Law is a very ancient translation, made in Egypt by learned men who had a good knowledge of the country. The geographical identifications thus represent the scholarship of a date which we may put more than two hundred years before the Christian Era, and tell us what was then thought in Egypt.

Generally, the Greek translation renders Goshen by Gesem or Gesen, but in one place it adds this mark of position, 'the land of Gesem of Arabia' (Gen. xlv. 10). It seems very strange to find an Arabia in Egypt, but we also find a Libya. The rich valley and plain formed the boundary between the great deserts of the East and the West, between Arabia and Libya. Thus one of the most eastern districts was called the nome or province of Arabia, and one of the most western that of Libya, as though they had been won by the fertilising Nile from the wastes on either side of the land it waters. This Arabia of the Greek translation is the Arabian Nome. Goshen was part of it, so the phrase 'Gesem of Arabia' implies. Leaving this question for the moment, we note that the Arabian Nome was bordered by that of Zoan on the north (the Tanite Nome), the field of Zoan being the nearest part of that neighbouring province. This explains the emphasis laid on the 'wonders in the field of Zoan.' The eastern position of the Arabian Nome suited it for the Hebrew settlement, for it held a border Shemite population, and lay outside the purely Egyptian territory, where shepherds were hateful (Gen. xlvi. 34). Other passages show that the old translators were a little perplexed with the geography of the district. Many changes had taken place, and much had been forgotten in a period of a thousand years : it is enough that they fixed their eyes on the Arabian Nome as the scene of the sojourn.

Dr. Brugsch has found the ancient Egyptian name of Goshen. It is Kesem or Pa-Kesem, the capital of the Arabian Nome, one reading transcribing the Hebrew Goshen with sufficient exactness, the other the classical Phaccusa. Thus there was a town as well as a land of Goshen. Why then was Goshen in Arabia, Gesem of Arabia, part, not the whole of the Nome? This is because the old province was twofold, so that when it was at last officially divided, the territory of Goshen remained attached to the chief town of the same name in the limited Arabian Nome, the other portion being separated as another province. This division actually took place under the Ptolemies; and it is at once a note of time, and a curious mark of accuracy, that the translators of the Septuagint, writing before the division, indicate Goshen as part of the Arabian Nome. It is remarkable, too, that, while they knew this much, they could not tell which part was the old Hebrew settlement, for it seems from two passages that they identified the land of Goshen with the part that was ultimately cut off, in spite of the part that remained carrying with it the old capital. All this detail may seem very tiresome, but it is really very important. It gives us two great results. When we do not know where the events of history happened, they become vague; moving, as it were, from place to place, they lose their strength of outline and distinctness of colour; no sooner are they fixed than they become real.

This is what we feel with startling force as we actually see Mount Carmel and Gilboa when the coast of Palestine rises before our view. But this is not all. As we fix the town of Goshen, the centre of the administration of the land of Goshen, we know where to dig for the Egyptian records of the Hebrew sojourn. The town is not a mere symbol in ancient maps; its name still survives on the old site, where extensive mounds bear witness to its former wealth. There, a little below the earth that we are too indifferent to turn, lie countless fragments of history, probably documents of the rule of Joseph and of the age of the Oppression.

Thus we can place the land of Goshen on the map, with the chief town of the same name. In the case of the town this was its civil name, which, as often happens in the border-land, was not Egyptian but Hebrew. There was another land of Goshen, conquered by Joshua, in southern Palestine (Josh. x. 41; xi. 16). The meaning of the name is doubtful; perhaps it is 'watered by rain,' and thus 'fertile,' the first sense suited to Palestine and the second to Egypt. Eastern settlers would have carried the name of a favoured territory with them, and given it to a new home. The sacred name of the town was Pe-Supt, the Abode of the god Supt: this we find in the Assyrian records in the form Pasupti, as the capital of one of the little kingdoms under which Egypt was divided from the middle of the eighth to the middle of the seventh century before the Christian Era. The local divinity Supt was a form of Horus, the sun of the day, and his sacred animal was probably the hawk. Supt was reverenced as the protector of the frontier, the subduer of the Shepherds. This was the Egyptian notion. Yet they had another view of this god as an object of worship of the stranger population. We see him represented as a Shemite divinity, with a foreign type of face and a foreign dress. Thus he is connected with the local religion of the Shepherds. We already saw in the history of Zoan that the Shepherds adored a divinity of their own whom the Egyptians identified with Set or Typhon. We now learn of another of their gods. Supt is connected with other foreign divinities worshipped in eastern Egypt, and consequently those of the Shepherds. They are alluded to in a curious passage in Amos (v. 25, 26, comp. Acts vii. 42, 43).

Not a vestige of the local worship of Goshen appears to have clung to the Hebrew nation after the conquest of Palestine. Moses and Joshua must surely have put it down with a strong hand. But it lasted long enough to pass into history; and so we learn that the religion of the Hebrews did not grow from an old idolatry of their own, a tribal worship, for the old idolatry of the Israelites in Egypt has no connection with the true Hebrew belief. It fell from its opposition to that belief, which has nothing whatever in common with it. Let this be well remembered.

As yet the early story of Goshen, land and city, is alone told in the Bible; we wait for the buried records before we can supply the commentary and fill up the gaps. Here Jacob came, bowed down with sorrow and age, to pass his last days near the great and prosperous son who ruled Egypt from the city of Zoan. An Egyptian wall-painting of the age of the Twelfth Dynasty, in a tomb at Benee-Hasan, pictures the coming of a Shemite family to settle in Egypt, a people different from the natives of the land, more fully and more richly clad, armed, and one like a true Hebrew playing as he goes on a musical instrument, the lyre. Asses bear the children and the scanty goods. The women come too. It is a real settlement. So journeyed the old patriarch till he was met by Joseph's wagons. So marched his turbulent sons, bearing their weapons of war, and maybe not without the music to which they sang the old songs that have perished.

The Hebrews settled. In due course Jacob died,

and was borne forth by the powerful governor with a mighty cavalcade, mummied as an Egyptian, and mourned with the customary wailing of Egypt, across the border to the ancient sepulchre which Abraham had bought, the cave wherein his fathers and sad Leah already rested. And Joseph died, and he could not be carried out; the power of the Shepherds was waning. So he took an oath of his people that they would take his bones with them when God should lead them forth. Thus he too was mummied, and the oath was remembered by Moses.

With the death of Joseph a great obscurity falls on the story of Goshen. Israel abode in Egypt four hundred and thirty years. At the death of Joseph we have only reached the close of the first seventy years, and are probably near the beginning of the Oppression. The great heat of the Oppression filled at least the last eighty years of the sojourn, from the birth of Moses to the Exodus. Of the time between Joseph's death and the birth of Moses we have but a solitary fact, the pathetic story of how all Ephraim's sons were cut off by the men of Gath born in Egypt, because of a cattle-lifting, on the part of Israelites or Gittites we cannot tell (1 Chron. vii. 20-22). It is a glimpse of a lawless and a troubled age. This is the time of which we long to know the history, and need not perhaps long in vain.

The darkness lifts, and Goshen has again a place in

history in the lively picture of the terrible Oppression and the great deliverance. Not that all the events here took place. The policy of Pharaoh was to scatter the people. Yet Goshen always remained their central home, and from it they went forth on the night of the Passover.

Again history is silent till the chief town is once more of note, when, as already said, it became the capital of one of the petty kings who divided Egypt among them in the days of the Ethiopian supremacy. Later still, under the Greek sovereigns, the place was a rich emporium of Asiatic trade.

Of the present site only this can be said, that, like many famous towns of Egypt, it is marked by extensive mounds, and a scattered modern village, still preserving the Greek form of the name, Fakoos, a little altered from Phaccusa. The country around is yet fertile, though the dwindled Nile-stream and neglected canals do not enrich it as of old. Imagination only can picture the prosperity that has passed away.

CHAPTER VII.

PITHOM.

To repeat in brief what has been already shown,—the building by the Hebrews of the 'treasure' cities or, better, 'store' cities (comp. 2 Chron. xxxii. 28), Pithom and Raamses (Exod. i. 11) or Rameses, seems to mark the beginning of the heat of the Oppression. The name Rameses points to Ramses II. as the great oppressor. The date was about B.C. 1400, some eighty years before the Exodus. After the expulsion of the Shepherds, who protected the Israelites, the settlers became a serf population. With the accession of Ramses a new policy began. The border and the foreign provinces were now organised upon a more settled basis of government than before; great forts were built to command the frontier; emporiums of trade were constructed. The growing multitudes of the Hebrews caused uneasiness to the Egyptian king, and their employment offered both a means of carrying out his great building projects, and of depriving the serfs of nationality and the power of combination.

Rameses or Zoan, we have seen, was a great centre of trade. Pithom, though we do not exactly know its site, lay within the border, and on or near the line of traffic by land. Thus both were store-cities rather than forts. We need not return to Rameses: Pithom is our present subject. Unfortunately, the Egyptian records tell us little of this town. Its sacred name in hieroglyphics is Pe-tum, the abode of Tum, the setting sun. The civil name was Tekut, which Dr. Brugsch identifies with the Succoth of the Bible, a conclusion which may be doubted. It was the capital of the Sethroïte Nome, the easternmost province of Lower Egypt. Though the site is not yet fixed, we can have little doubt that it is marked by one of the many mounds which lie in this unexplored territory.

Round the subject of Pithom and Rameses, a great French scholar, the lamented M. Chabas (*Mélanges*, 2me sér. p. 108 foll.), has grouped all the scattered illustrations of the Oppression which the Egyptian records afford. They are disappointing in their scantiness, and from the absence of precise mention of the Hebrews. This seems at first sight very strange. Of the reign of Ramses II., now held to be the great oppressor, there are abundant records; that of his son Menptah, identified with the Pharaoh of the Exodus, is less amply represented. The inscriptions of both taken together, and of their great officers, and the correspondence and memoranda of the scribes, would fill volumes. But when we come to look into these documents, we find that they cover a very limited space of the field which we call history. The kings record their conquests and their donations to the temples; the officers deal with their personal services to the crown, and the posts which they held; the scribes give us official correspondence. There is no history of the people of Egypt, or of the strangers in the land. That which modern history claims as its most interesting province is here omitted, or told only by accident, as when some detail of the life of the subjects appears in connection with a command which a scribe orders or executes. It is thus that the darkness clears now and again, and we see the same picture of oppression whch the Bible portrays, the heavy forced labour of multitudes toiling in the heat of the furnace of iron.

In these fragmentary notices the Hebrews are not mentioned by name. M. Chabas indeed thought that he had discovered them in a foreign serf population, the Aperiu, whose name is not very different from that of the Hebrews in their own language, with the important exception that the change from b to p is most unlikely. The identification was hailed with delight, but by degrees difficulties presented themselves. First of all it was found that there were still Aperiu in Egypt more than half a century after the Exodus : these might perhaps be a fragment of the people who stayed behind. Next it was discovered that some were horsemen, which the Hebrews never were ; and last of all, that they were employed in public works before the Israelites came into Egypt. Yet the name is so often used for foreign bondsmen engaged in the very work of the Hebrews, and especially during the Oppression, that it is hard not to believe it to be a general term in which they are included though it does not actually describe them.

The most precious pictorial illustration of the Oppression is a wall-painting in a tomb at Thebes, showing prisoners taken in war by Thothmes III. engaged in building some parts of the great temple of Amen. The date is long before the building of Rameses, perhaps a century and a half. The labourers are captives, not serfs, yet they are clearly Shemites, kinsfolk of the Hebrews, and the work they are doing is the same as that of the Hebrews, and organised in the same manner.

In the painting, we first see the captives drawing water in jars from a deep tank in which lotus-lilies are blooming, and around which trees are planted. Others are engaged in breaking up masses of earth with hoes. Others carry the moistened clay, which their comrades place in wooden forms, and arrange the shaped bricks in rows to dry in the sun. The bricks when dried are stacked, and carried where needed in slings suspended from yokes. Another gang bears stone and mortar; and at the end of the scene is a carefully-constructed wall topped and partly faced with stone. One overseer, with his staff under his arm, sits watching; another, staff in hand, follows the labourers. Dr. Brugsch reads the main inscription, '(Here are seen) the captives who were carried away as living prisoners in very great numbers: they work at the building with dexterous fingers; their overseers show themselves in sight; these attend with strictness, obeying the orders of the great skilful lord (who prescribes to them) the works, and gives directions to the masters. (They are rewarded) with wine and all kinds of good dishes; they perform their service with a mind full of love for the king; they build for Thothmes III. a holy of holies for (the gods) ; may it be rewarded to him through a range of many endless years.' The overseer is made to say, 'The stick is in my hand, be not idle.' Very aptly Dr. Brugsch quotes these two passages of Scripture : 'They did set over them taskmasters (superintendents of works) to afflict them with their burdens' (Exod. i. 11); 'And the taskmasters hasted (them), saying, Fulfil your works, (your) daily tasks' (v. 13). Pharaoh's retort to the complaint of the Hebrew overseers, 'Ye (are) idle, idle' (ver. 17), is even more pointedly illustrative of the text of our picture.

These captives were engaged in two separate labours, the building of a provision-house, and of a sanctuary. (Brugsch, 'History,' 2 ed. i., p. 417 foll.) The chief work here is brick-making and building with bricks. In the narrative of Exodus, nothing is said of any other labour : quarrying is, however, mentioned traditionally. The great bulk of Egyptian building was with brick;

houses, forts, circuit-walls of towns and temples, were all in this material, and the mason's labour was almost limited to temples and tombs.

The climate of Egypt does not make it necessary to burn the bricks. In the present day, unburnt brick is in common use in the villages, except near the northern coast, where rain is not infrequent. The bricks are merely shaped and placed in the sun to dry. Anciently this was done with more skill and care than now. The oldest bricks, as in the case of those of the brick pyramids in the Necropolis of Memphis, are, as a rule, bound with pebbles and similar materials, while the later bricks of the age of the Empire are bound with straw. This fact disposes of the old fancy that the Israelites laboured for the kings who built the pyramids. The brick-mould or form was very carefully made : it was of wood, and sometimes bore on its inner face the name of the sovereign under whose orders it was used. Thus we can frequently date Egyptian buildings from the royal names occurring on the bricks, precisely as we can date those of Assyria and Babylonia from the bricks which are more frequently stamped in the same manner.

The Bible mentions three degrees of officers who

controlled the Israelites, of whom one class only is seen in the wall-picture. The whole scheme of the Oppression was entrusted to superior taskmasters, who are called 'superintendents of works' (Exod. i. 11). These seem to have organised the labour, for they do not afterwards appear in the details of the narrative, in which we read of taskmasters, probably Egyptians, and overseers, certainly Israelites (v. 6, foll.). The taskmasters superintended the work staff in hand (comp. ver. 14), and the overseers were merely selected labourers who acted as interpreters and chiefs of gangs, and were beaten, in the event of failure, like the common workmen. While the wall-painting only represents the ordinary Egyptian taskmaster, the occupant of the tomb the chapel of which it adorns was probably one of the higher superintendents.

A still closer agreement with the Scripture narrative is found in the memorandum of a scribe of the age of the great Oppression, which states that twelve men engaged in the fields in making bricks, having neglected their task, 'of producing their tale of bricks every day,' were set to work in building a house, and it is added that their toil was not to be relaxed. Nothing could be more exact. Similarly we read of the allowance of grain for the Aperiu who were engaged in forced labour.

One more illustration of the sojourn may be drawn from the group of documents belonging to the same period. It is a note of the authorisation given by Menptah, the Pharaoh of the Exodus, to certain Arab chiefs of Edom, to settle near Pithom ' in order that they and their cattle might live in the great farm of Pharaoh.' This, as M. Chabas points out, is precisely parallel to the settlement of Jacob and his family. It may be added that it is not impossible that these strangers were invited, or allowed to come, in order that they might take the place of the Israelites scattered in their labour, and thus break up the nationality of the Hebrew settlement.

Scanty as these illustrations are, it will be seen that they show the accuracy of the narrative in the Bible. Any day may afford such direct evidence as has been hoped for ever since hieroglyphics were interpreted. Explorations in Egypt, especially in the sites of the Land of Goshen and the neighbourhood, may yield the wished-for result, or it may be found in some neglected papyrus, perhaps a mere fragment, in a small museum or a private collection. A few lines scrawled by an Egyptian scribe, the memorandum of what he thought an indifferent everyday transaction, may be deciphered, and tell us of the Hebrews by name, or even mention some name already known to us from the Scripture narrative.

CHAPTER VIII.

MIGDOL.

THE route of the Israelites out of Egypt to the sea which they crossed is hard to trace. Nature, war, and neglect have changed the face of the country, and swept away the ancient landmarks. The traveller who journeys on his camel to Palestine may follow the footsteps of the Hebrews, but he knows it not; the steamer which carries her busy or careless freight of modern men up the Canal of Suez must somewhere cut the very path of the Exodus, but where none can tell. Sea and land are not where they were three thousand years ago. The coast line of the Mediterranean has little changed, but the Lake Menzeleh behind it has very greatly increased. The Red Sea has retired many miles. As the prophet foretold, the tongue of the Egyptian Sea, the head of the Gulf of Suez, has been dried up (Isa. xi. 15, comp. xix. 5). The territory submerged by Lake Menzeleh can be seen by the maps laid down on the authority of classical geographers. In the time of Strabo, three branches of the Nile, the Mendesian, Tanitic, and Pelusiac, all flowed into the Mediterranean. The meres that lay at that time between these channels have now merged in the one great lake, in whose widespread waters the Nile-streams are lost. These waters are spread over the fields, the orchards, and the vineyards of whole provinces; while the islets bear the mounds of long-forgotten cities once on the highroads of traffic. The roads which the Roman Itinerary of Antoninus shows connecting Pelusium with Tanis (Zoan) and with Daphnæ, more to the south, are obliterated in the morasses. The fertile land through which the Hebrews passed in their first two stages, is now a desolation, uninhabited and untended; in the season of the inundation a morass, an extension of Lake Menzeleh peopled alone by countless flocks of wild fowl; for the rest of the year, a stretch of dry mud, cracked by the burning heat of the sun, a grey wilderness more dreary even than the yellow wilderness which bounds it on the east. For the desert of the third stage of the march is, as of old, an expanse of shifting sand, unlike the rocky desert to the south. It is only varied by the drifts, which form low hills. Beyond the third stage, to the northeast, stretches the Lake Serbonis, which has been at times, as now, a sheet of water, at times a dangerous morass, treacherously veiled by the wind-swept sand, which indeed still covers its southern limits. The frontier-wall has disappeared, with its forts, but the eastward road, whereby the great armies of Egypt went to war in Syria, is yet followed by the caravans, which pass mounds, each hiding one of the ancient castles of the Pharaohs. The great wall and the forts, built of crude brick, have crumbled into the plain, and been buried by the drifting sand. It would be a costly labour to unveil the remains hidden by the mounds, but the result would be the recovery of many a lost chapter of history.

It would seem hopeless to trace the Israelite route along this land of oblivion. The map has been washed out by the waters and worn out by the sand. And if we could follow the emigrants to what was the shore of the sea, that sea has withdrawn. Yet the work is not so hard as it appears. It needs patience and a wise separation of fact from conjecture. We know the two most important points of the great journey, and from them we may find the direction of the march. The departure was from Rameses, identified, as already shown, with the great city of Zoan, still retaining its name in the Arabic Sán. The last encampment before the sea was crossed was near Migdol, and Migdol is so well fixed by classical evidence that we may venture to say which mound in the desert covers its remains. If we cannot point to the sites of the two intermediate stations, Succoth and Etham, we can draw a line from Zoan to Migdol, making allowance in its direction for the difficulties of the country, less in the age of the Exodus than now, and we cannot be far wrong.

We have, however, much more than this to do. Where was the sea at this time? Did it extend to near Migdol, of which we know the site, and was it the Red Sea? For as we look at the map, though we can trace a chain of lakes and marshes between the south-eastern angle of Lake Menzeleh and the Red Sea at Suez, we must ascertain which of these represents the utmost northern extension, in historical times, of the Gulf of Suez, which now has its head at the town whence it takes its name. When this is done, we must try and see how far in this direction the sea extended in the days of Moses, three thousand years ago.

We cannot always trace the causes of the changes we notice in the extent of sea and land. We know, however, that gulfs are filled up by rivers and the sea, or by the sea alone. Rivers, bringing down alluvial matter, form deltas at their mouths, like the Nile and the Mississippi. The sea aids them by silting up sand from its bed. Even in historical times, the Euphrates and Tigris, aided by the Persian Gulf, have filled up the vast space between the present sea-shore and Ur of the Chaldees, which four thousand years ago was a port from whose terraced pyramid were seen the ancient ships which went to and fro on the Indian trade over the waters now covered by dreary marsh-land, the perpetual home of the plague. Here we trace a double agency. Where there is no great river, the sea alone does the work, unless there is also volcanic action. This last agency we may perhaps omit in speaking of the Gulf of Suez, for ordinary silting is enough to account for what we see.

It may make the subject easier if we think of changes on our own coast which are still going on. On the south of Sussex we notice that gradual retirement of the sea, which has ruined Winchelsea and impoverished Rye. Beyond the historic limits we may trace still more ancient shore-lines at higher levels. The whole fen-country is an instance of the same reclamation of land on a much larger scale. Not that this has been regular and without intermission for ages. We must remember that once the Channel was bridged by an isthmus, and Britain and Gaul were one, just as north-western Africa was joined to Spain at the very time when the Great Desert, the Sahara, was a sea. We need not, however, perplex ourselves with remote geological conditions, but bear in mind only that gulfs and bays are generally filled up by the work of water agencies. The case of the Egyptian Delta is an exception. It was indeed won from the sea, yet the sea, or at least the water, has since with success claimed back part of its old domain: but of this later.

Looking at the chain of lakes on the map, we have no difficulty in tracing three distinct pieces of water. Nearest Suez is the marsh called the Bitter Lakes, then Lake Timsáh, and lastly Lake Balláh, on the north-east of which is the site of Migdol. Not far northward is the south-eastern extension of Lake Menzeleh. Without historical evidence, it would be impossible to say whether these waters were once part of the Red Sea or of the Mediterranean, or to which sea we should assign some or all of them. All we could infer would be that at some time there was a communication between the lakes. But the evidence we want is at hand.

The Greek geographer Strabo, a very accurate writer, tells us that the town of Heroönpolis was in the angle of the Arabian Gulf or Gulf of Suez, which Pliny a little later calls, after the town, the Heroöpolite Gulf. This place must have stood on the north-west of the present Lake Timsáh, not far from the town of Isma'eel-eeyeh (Ismailia), the modern inland port of the Suez Canal. Thus in Strabo's time, about nineteen centuries ago, the Gulf extended over forty miles northward of its present head at Suez.

This view has been combated on account of the discovery of the line of an old canal running from Suez northwards for more than twelve miles. The date of this canal cannot be fixed. If it is of the time of the Pharaohs, it must have been cut through the silt which obstructed the sea between Suez and the Bitter Lakes.

Strabo says that in his time people embarked at Heroönpolis for the voyage down the Red Sea. Thus though it may have been necessary, in an earlier age, to unite the broad parts of the Gulf by a canal, the head of the Gulf was then still placed near Heroönpolis. If so the inhabitants of Egypt had not forgotten the former extension of the sea.

Heroönpolis, however, is over twenty miles farther south than Migdol, as we know from a Roman document giving the distances on the military roads, the Itinerary of Antoninus. Did the Red Sea between the time of Moses and that of Strabo retire this distance? In other words, is the marsh Lake Balláh, which is the shrunken representative of a larger expanse of water, and even now extends in a narrow arm almost as far as the site of Migdol, the representative of the head of the Gulf at the time of Moses? Before we answer this question we must put another. Could the Gulf at any historical time extend beyond Heroönpolis northwards? Where are we to draw the line of separation in the chain of lakes between the domain of the Red Sea and that of the Mediterranean? The levels taken for the cutting of the Suez Canal would seem at first sight to fix the limits of the former Gulf of Suez where they were in Strabo's time, at the north of Lake Timsáh, and to assign Lake Balláh to the Mediterranean system with which it is now in connection. Between the two is the sandy elevation of El-Gisr, rising in one place about forty, in another about fifty feet, above the level of the Red Sea at Suez, which is ten feet above that of the Mediterranean. This elevation, to cut the canal through which was an arduous labour, is not throughout a marine deposit. The lowest part of one section reveals a tough bed at the base above the Suez level. The rest is wholly of sand, and might easily have been accumulated by drifts. Thus the obstacle is not serious, but it does not seem to have covered a recent sea-bed. If we look at any large map, we perceive that the ancient extension of Lake Timsáh could have avoided this tract, and passed round it to the westward, where the levels are low. The engineers of a direct canal had to face the difficulty, and overcame it bravely.

Thus there is no reason why the Gulf of Suez should not have extended, in historical times, so far north as to include Lake Balláh; yet we could not be sure of this were it not for a curious piece of evidence. The great

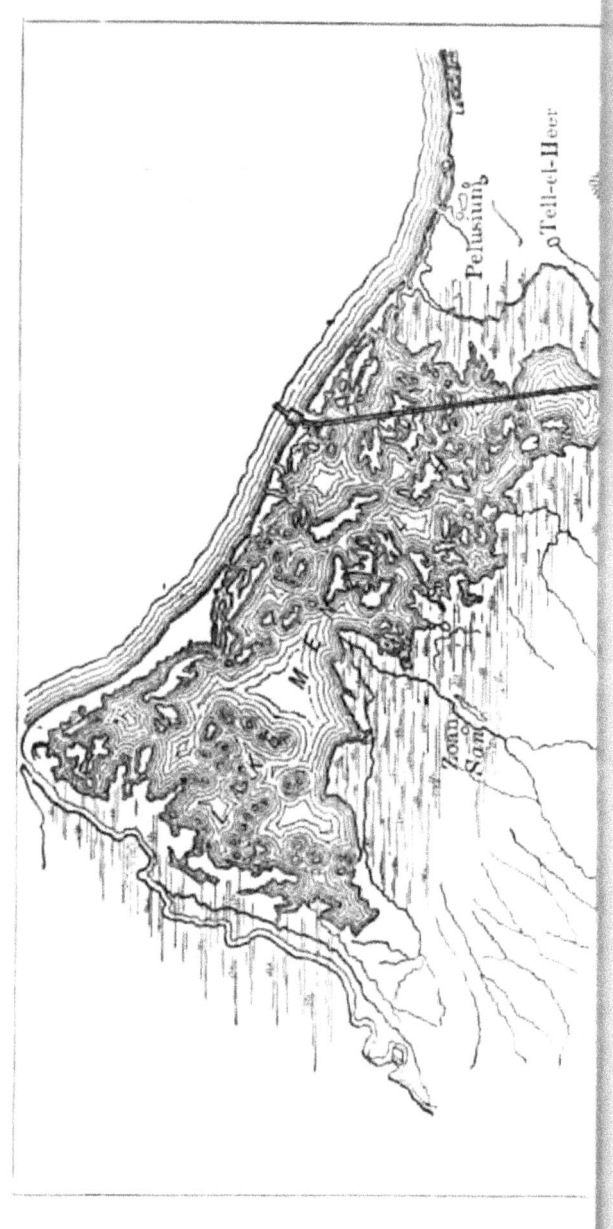

caravan route to Palestine now passes to the north of the lake. It is the old Egyptian military road. This is attested by the mounds which define its course, the remains of the ancient stations. Obviously the Pharaohs would have chosen the best line of march, north of the Red Sea, and so between the two seas.

A word must be said of the Mediterranean and the lakes which are fed by it and by the Nile, the great backwaters on the northern coast, for the route of the Exodus must have depended on the condition of the country between the starting-point and the sea to be crossed. Here again we see a startling change of level. The rise of the land on the south of the Isthmus of Suez has been balanced by a fall on the north. We have said that Lake Menzeleh has swallowed up the populous and fertile tract which once stretched around the meres from which it has grown, and along the Nile streams. But to show that there is no conjecture here we must speak for a moment of the recent geological history of the northern part of the Delta.

In spite of the change within, the coast-line of the Mediterranean seems to have scarcely varied in historical times. The depression has taken place in the long range of lakes. The outline of the Delta has remained the same. The Nile, aided by the action of the sea, at first filled up the great gulf which the Delta occupies, and pushed a blunt wedge of land into the ocean northwards. Probably currents sweeping along the coast, and the want of good holding-ground for deposit, arrested the farther conquest of the domain of the sea. But this does not explain the loss of ground by the land in the lakes. We should rather have expected that they would have been filled up by the deposit of the Nile, especially since the channels have been reduced from seven to two. For instead of seven branches pouring the alluvial deposit into the sea, only two do so, and most of the rest empty themselves in the lakes. Of course something is due to neglect of the dykes, and to war. Thus the westernmost of the lakes, Mareotis, had dried up when the British army cut a dam and filled it once more, for military purposes, at the siege of Alexandria in the beginning of this century; since when the great port has been unhealthy. We cannot explain the general process, which is most remarkably seen in Lake Menzeleh, unless we suppose a gradual fall of the land, at least in the north of the Isthmus of Suez, and a corresponding rise in the south.

It is important here to notice that the long narrow lake which is the most eastern of the whole series of backwaters, the ancient Lake Serbonis, does not seem to have changed its shape since the time of the classical geographers. Its southern shore is protected by sand hills, and it is free from the disturbing element of the Nile streams. Unlike the rest, it is fed only by the ocean.

The place of Migdol may be determined by the evidence already alluded to, that of the Itinerary of Antoninus, according to which it stood at a distance of twelve Roman miles from Pelusium. This would fix its site at the mound now called Tell-es-Samoot, where Dr. Brugsch places it. The modern name preserves the ancient Egyptian Samut.

Migdol is mentioned in the Bible as near the third camping-place of the Israelites (Exod. xiv. 2; Numb. xxxiii. 7). The Hebrew name Migdol recurs in the Maktal of the Egyptian monuments, the place having, like Zoan, a double name, one Semitic and the other (Samut) Egyptian. The classical form is Magdolos or Magdolon. In an inscription of a king of the Eighteenth Dynasty, Dr. Brugsch finds the limits of Egypt defined as from Elephantine to Samut (Hist. i. p. 498). Similarly

Ezekiel speaks of these limits 'from Migdol to Syene' (xxix. 10, xxx. 6, *margin*). Elephantine is an island opposite to Syene, the border-town on the south; Samut, as just remarked, still holds its place on the map. The name of Migdol implies that it was a fort, but a town must have grown around it, for it received a colony of fugitive Jews in the time of Jeremiah (xliv. 1). Under the Pharaohs it had been apparently the most important fort on the eastern frontier, but in the later days of the monarchy, the great danger of attack by sea raised the consequence of Pelusium or Sin, which became 'the strength of Egypt' (Ezek. xxx. 15).

We will now endeavour to trace the Israelite route on the map. From Zoan to near Migdol the distance in a straight line does not exceed thirty miles. As Mr. Greville Chester has remarked, a much directer course could have been followed at the time of the Exodus than is now possible, if (as is certain), Lake Menzeleh was anciently far less extensive (Quarterly Statement Palestine Exploration Fund, July 1880, p. 146). Ten or twelve miles a day would be as much as the Israelites could accomplish. The journey was not through 'the way of the land of the Philistines, although that (was) near'

(Exod. xiii. 17). This confirms the identification of Migdol with Magdolos. Having reached that point, the natural course would have been to turn eastward to Pelusium, and follow the coast-road leading to the Philistine country; but there was danger of war (Exod. l. c.), and therefore the Hebrews were commanded to 'return and encamp before Pi-hahiroth, between Migdol and the sea, over against Baal-zephon.' They were to encamp by the sea, and Pharaoh would suppose that they were entangled in the land, and shut in by the wilderness (Exod. xiv. 2, 3). We cannot identify either Pi-hahiroth or Baal-zephon. Dr. Brugsch, however, thinks with reason that Pi-hahiroth should be read 'the mouth of the abysses,' indicating a place of quicksands. Baal-zephon was no doubt the seat of the worship of a 'Baal of the north,' a name which tells us to look for this site in the north of the isthmus. The worship of Baal did not extend to the south of Egypt; the north of its eastern territory is thus implied.

The position of Migdol is at first perplexing. The encampment between Migdol and the sea would be rather to the north-east than, as we should have expected, to the west of the ancient head of the gulf.

Two suppositions may explain this. The gulf may have turned eastwards beyond where we can now trace it, and passed to the southward of Migdol, a view which agrees with the statement that the sea was driven back by the strong east wind, which implies a sea flowing from west to east as here supposed. In this case the Israelites would have crossed from north to south. This question can never be settled without a survey. On the other hand, the obvious strategy of Pharaoh would have been to wheel the left wing of his chariot-force and throw it across the road to Palestine which the Israelites had left to the north, and this movement might have forced them back along the west side of the gulf if it ran northward, and they would have ultimately crossed from west to east. In this case the east wind would have divided the sea, and not literally driven it back.

It is perhaps best to leave the majestic old narrative without farther discussion. The sea has disappeared, and curiosity cannot measure the depth. Like the burial-place of Moses, the scene of the great deliverance is unknown. It is enough that the conditions of the country confirm the historical truth of the narrative, while they baffle the inquiries of the critic.

'Thy way (was) in the sea, and thy path in the great waters, and thy footsteps were not known (Psalm lxxvii. 19).[1]

The able German scholar, Dr. Brugsch, who has more than any one illustrated the story of Israel in Egypt, astonished the Oriental Congress held at London in 1874, with a theory of the route of the Exodus, which if not new was enforced by a mass of new and curious evidence. The idea that the Israelites did not cross the Red Sea, but passed along the narrow and treacherous way between Lake Serbonis and the Mediterranean, had been already suggested by another learned German, Dr. Schleiden, in his book on the Isthmus of Suez (Die Landenge von Sués, 1858), but the brilliant revival of the theory has hidden its first advocate in undeserved oblivion. Having given him the credit due to an originator, we may speak of the theory as Dr. Brugsch's, since he has put it in the form best known to the public. His view is here adopted as far as the identification of Migdol, with a reserve as to the sites of the two previous encampments at Succoth and Etham. Pi-hahiroth he

[1] The reading is from the Queen's Printers' Bible (Sunday School Centenary Bible), which with the Aids to the Student gives the main results of the study of the text of Scripture.

places at the western end of the Serbonian Lake, and Baal-zephon he identifies with the temple of Zeus, or Jupiter, Casius on a headland, Mount Casius, in the strip of land between the Mediterranean and the lake. The objection to these identifications is that whereas in the Bible Migdol, Pi-hahiroth, and Baal-zephon, are all spoken of as together, Dr. Brugsch puts Migdol and Baal-zephon as far apart as Zoan and Migdol, and thus he makes the last day's march as long as the three preceding stages. Again, he makes the change of route to avoid the way of the Philistines, from the headland of Mount Casius across the Serbonian Lake by an isthmus. But the change took place before the last encampment near Migdol, not after it, and Mr. Greville Chester has shown that Dr. Brugsch's isthmus is purely imaginary. He travelled by the strip of coast to test the theory, and found it failed (Quart. Statement Pal. Ex. Fund, July 1880, p. 154). So far for the sites. With respect to the event, Dr. Brugsch holds that the Israelites passed between the sea and the lake by a practicable route, whereas the Egyptian army perished by the overflow of the ocean, an event of extremely rare occurrence; and this view seems contrary to the narrative in Exodus. But it is a mistake into which he has himself fallen, to suppose that the miracle could thus be explained away. We cannot attempt to define this or that cause as the essential part of a miracle : it is best to view the event in its completeness and, in this instance, to bear in mind the opportuneness of the conditions needed for the passage of the Israelites and for the overthrow of their pursuers.

In his 'Dictionnaire Géographique,' Dr. Brugsch seems to abandon the farther part of his route, and to place the scene of the Exodus in the swamps of the south-east of Lake Menzeleh, but he has not defined this view.

To return for a moment to the explanation offered in this chapter : it is confirmatory of its accuracy to see that the Israelites came on the third day to the 'bitter' waters of Marah, for in their southward journey about thirty miles would bring them to the Bitter Lakes ; and this is in agreement with the supposed rate of march to Migdol.

When we reflect on the vast period of time which has passed since the Exodus, three thousand years, or ninety generations of men, we may well wonder that any of the places mentioned in the ancient narrative can yet be most. When we recollect what changes time and war have wrought, it is still more marvellous. There has been no other history but that of the Bible, and this we have to place side by side with monuments which say nothing of the event. Tradition does not help, but misleads us. Yet enough remains, even without moving the sand for the historical treasures it conceals, to enable us to restore the main outlines of the map of the Exodus. Future research may tell us more, but we can scarcely doubt that to the end of time the actual place of the passage of the Red Sea will remain a mystery.

CHAPTER IX.

ON.

A SOLITARY obelisk of red granite, set up at least four thousand years ago, alone marks the site of On, also called the City of the Sun, in Hebrew Beth-shemesh, in Greek Heliopolis (*see* p. 134). Nothing else can be seen of the splendid shrine and the renowned university which were the former glories of the place. Amid the memories of the site, a fable told to the Greek and Roman visitors makes the solitude vocal with a lesson of instruction. Here was wont to come, once in five hundred years or more, that mysterious Arabian bird, the phœnix. The winged wonder had no sooner settled than he made his nest, only to set it in flames and perish, when lo! from his ashes arose a new phœnix, which spread his red and golden wings and flew away to the unknown land whence his parent came. The priests, after their manner, spoke in allegories. What they would have taught we can only guess. They may have intended the conjunction of the solar year with their wandering year, which, as it wanted the intercalary day, was always losing time, and went back through the seasons of nature. They may have figured the resurrection. Learned men have interpreted the riddle one way, the Fathers of the Church the other. To us the story is fittest as a type of the wisdom of the Egyptians, which at Heliopolis had a chosen seat for thousands of years. The university to which the wise men of Greece resorted perished when a new centre of knowledge was founded in the Greek city of Alexandria. It did not decay; it was destroyed: the schools were carried away or closed for want of students, and most of the splendid obelisks were transplanted. But the old learning lived again in fresh vigour in its second home. In due course the university of Alexandria waned and vanished, but not until it had reappeared in another phase, at Baghdad and Cordova, under the protection of the Arabs. For centuries, while the rest of the world was dark, these and the kindred schools handed on the unextinguished torch. At last they too disappeared, at the very moment when their scholars had provided successors in the great cities of Christendom. Not a link is wanting in this long chain ; though, as we visit Naples and Bologna, Paris, Oxford, and Cambridge, little do we think of the forgotten parent who rests in the mouldering ruins where the single obelisk still points heavenwards, while in the carved hieroglyphics of its sides the wild bees, types of the industry of scholars, make their nests.

The origin of both city and university at On is unknown ; but there is good reason for carrying both back to the very dawn of Egyptian history. Probably their foundation was earlier than that of Memphis ; and Memphis was built by Menes, the first king of Egypt. In the order of the great gods, the chief objects of worship, we trace the union of the system of Abydos in Upper Egypt with that of Heliopolis in Lower Egypt. Abydos was close to This, or Thinis, the primitive capital of Menes, abandoned for Memphis ; Heliopolis lay near the new city. The ancient king seems, when he united the government of the two divisions of the country, to have combined the pantheons of two great seats of religion. The position of the old city does not seem to have been chosen for any political reason ; it commands no pass ; yet there were times in the history of Egypt when Heliopolis, as the nearest place north of Memphis on the great eastern road, gained some military consequence; but this was a mere accident, due to the weakness of the state.

The civil name of the town was An, the Hebrew On, the sacred name, Pe-Ra, 'the Abode of the Sun.' The religion was the worship of Ra, the sun, in different personified forms. The ideas of the sun of the day and that of the night, the visible and the invisible luminary, were reverenced as Munt and Tum. There were two cities called An, one in Upper, and the other in Lower Egypt, the southern the Hermonthis of the Greeks, and the northern their Heliopolis; and the solar worship was divided, Munt being worshipped at the one city, Tum at the other. Thus Tum, the sun of the night, was the special god of Heliopolis, though the ordinary general form of the sun, Ra, was also there worshipped, with other solar divinities. It seems that Ra had a temple, and Tum a separate edifice, perhaps a shrine. The sacred animals of the sun-gods, several, not one as usually elsewhere, were kept in the precincts. There was the black bull, Mnevis, apparently a lion and lioness, a cat, and the bennu, a crane, which was at once a living bird, and represented the mystical phœnix. This creature cannot have been the same as the bird of legend, for the inscriptions speak of the phœnix as living in a temple or shrine of his own at Heliopolis, and yet as the phœnix who creates himself. Here was also a sacred tree, the persea, on the fruits of which the gods are portrayed writing the name of the king. This accumulation of revered objects is peculiarly characteristic of the City of the Sun, and seems to show that it was a centre of Egyptian religion, representing far more than the local worship of other and greater cities.

In the story of the triumphal progress of Pianchi, the Ethiopian priest-king, who conquered Egypt about B.C. 750, there is a curious narrative of the royal visit to the shrines of Heliopolis. Coming towards the city, Pianchi reached Merti, the modern Matareeyeh, and purified himself in the basin of the cold spring, the famous Fountain of the Sun. He made a great offering to the Sun, at his rising, of white bulls, milk, perfume, incense, and all kinds of sweet-scented woods. He next went to the temple of Ra, and entered it, making two adorations. The priest invoked the divinity as the king's protector against his enemies. The king then fulfilled the rites of the door; he assumed the sacred garments (?); he purified himself with incense; he poured a libation; he carried the sacred flowers. Then he mounted the steps to the great sanctuary, to see Ra there; he went alone; he drew the bolt; he opened the doors; he saw his father Ra in the sanctuary; he adored the boat of Ra and the boat of Tum. He closed the doors, and sealed them with sealing-earth, stamped with the seal of the king. He then commanded the priests: 'I have placed my seal; let no other king enter there!' The priests prostrated themselves before the sovereign. He then entered the temple of Tum, and performed the sacred rites there also (De Rougé, 'Chrestomathie Égyptienne,' iv. pp. 58–61).

This narrative, taken almost word for word from the hieroglyphic tablet, gives us a curious glimpse into the most sacred rites of an Egyptian temple. The conqueror, be it remembered, was himself of the sacerdotal class, the descendant and representative of the high-priest-kings of Thebes. Hence his claim to enter the sanctuary of Ra, and his endeavour to exclude other kings. What was contained within the door of which he drew the bolt we can scarcely tell; certainly there were the arks or sacred boats, and perhaps a statue of Ra. In other temples, as at Dendarah, the arks were in a part of the edifice accessible to the priests, and carried in and out. There was no sacred animal in this sanctuary, otherwise it could not have been kept closed.

It is time to turn to the history of the City of the Sun. The oldest record is the fine obelisk, raised by Usurtesen I., of the Twelfth Dynasty, before the time of Abraham. We next read of the place in the history of Joseph, who married Asenath, daughter of Potipherah, priest of On (Gen. xli. 45, 50). The name, of which that of Potiphar may be another form, is found in Egyptian as Pet-p-ra, 'Belonging to Ra,' the Sun. It is thus specially appropriate to a priest of On. Again in the great papyrus of Ramses III., recording his donations to the temples of Egypt, those of Thebes, Memphis, and Heliopolis hold the most prominent places. The official inventory of the property of the temple is amazing, and well deserves a special essay. Later, in the days of the prophets, the splendour of the temples, adorned with many obelisks, is hinted at in the prediction of Jeremiah, that Nebuchadnezzar should break 'the pillars of Beth-shemesh,' distinguished as the Egyptian city from the three towns of the name in Palestine, and should burn the temples of the gods of the Egyptians (Jer. xliii. 13), so destroying the shrines of sun-worship with the very element there adored. Ezekiel notices the military importance of the place as standing on the way to Memphis, like Pi-beseth (Bubastis), foretelling the slaughter of their young men in Nebuchadnezzar's invasion (Ezek. xxx. 17). Here the name is pointed to read *aven*, vanity or idolatry ; but as the vowels were only inserted twelve centuries ago, this is probably a mere Rabbinical fancy. Without the vowels, the two words are the same; and the proper reading can only be decided by the general sense of the passages.

Just as the City of the Sun disappears from sacred history, it begins to be of interest in the story of the infancy of Greek philosophy. For centuries the restless tribes of Greece had been known to the Egyptians, first as pirates who descended on the northern coast, and then as mercenaries, ready to take any side for pay. Under the Saïte kings they became an important element in the army of the Pharaohs. In the same age they obtained commercial privileges, and had their great trading-station of Naucratis, in the north-west of the

Delta. This was in the time when their love of adventure took a fresh direction. They began to be curious about other lands, their products, and their wonders, and to seek the aid of older wisdom in the problems of the universe, to which the wise men turned their thoughts. Egypt was the nearest of the lands of primitive civilisation, and to Egypt the Greek philosophers journeyed, to question the priests on the subjects which captivated their minds. Here, if anywhere, would they find the tradition of the beginning of history, and even of the changes of the earth; here the long record of the movements of the heavenly bodies. Science had flourished for ages in the Egyptian schools; and Greeks came there to learn, whose disciples were to return as the teachers of the Egyptians. The first visitors were probably mere travellers, and met with a jealous reception. The priests did not care to tell their secrets to strangers, who could only speak through interpreters, and without hesitation asked them deep questions which they had scarcely ventured to look at even through the veil of mythological language. The inquirers went much deeper in speculation than the Egyptians, caring nothing for the limits set by local religious teaching. And even practical science was so mixed up in Egypt with sacred things, that the Greek separation of the two must have startled the conservative priests of Egypt. But in course of time there came a change; for when Greek was better known in Egypt, the priests' houses at Heliopolis were opened to at least the most distinguished inquirers. It was during the temporary independence of the country under native kings after the first Persian rule, that Plato the philosopher, and Eudoxus the mathematician, studied at Heliopolis. The geographer Strabo, when he visited Egypt shortly before the Christian Era, was shown as a sight the very houses where these illustrious strangers were lodged. The journey of Plato is nowhere related in any detail; but we have the story of that of Eudoxus. He had studied under Plato, but after he had been dismissed by him, his own friends paid his expenses to Egypt, and gave him letters of recommendation to Nectanabis, the reigning Pharaoh, who passed him on to the priests. He shaved his beard and conformed to their rule of life, and, after long study at Heliopolis, came away with advanced knowledge of astronomy. In his case we cannot doubt that Egyptian science was of value; rude as it was, it surpassed what the

Greeks had hitherto possessed. How far Plato benefited by his stay in Egypt we do not know. As, however, we learn more and more of the ideas of the Egyptians, we find the connection with Plato's notions of divine things more and more marked; nor are there wanting in his 'Dialogues' touches which show a personal knowledge of Egyptian character.

Probably it was at Heliopolis, or Hermopolis, which seems to have been the great university of the Empire, that Moses was educated in all the wisdom of the Egyptians. What, we ask, was the old instruction? This we can only discover from what the learned men knew; for we have no direct record of education. Just in the same way modern books give us the measure of the training of the learned in every country, though we do not question them, for it is simpler to consult the calendars of schools and universities.

First of all the Egyptian scribe must have learnt his own language, with its different forms of writing; and as it was expressed by pictures of objects, some letters, some syllables, some symbols, all of which in the finest style had to be beautifully drawn, this subject included some training in art. In the time of Moses, either

Hebrew, or a language akin to it, was also taught. The documents of the scribes of that age not only show by their accurate transliteration of Semitic words that the writers had a mastery of the foreign sounds they wrote; but more than this, it was, as already noticed, the fashion at this time to introduce Semitic words into the Egyptian language. The sacred books, voluminous and hard to interpret, were also studied by those who intended to follow the career of priests. Some science was taught. Astronomy was necessary for the calendar, and closely connected with religion. Arithmetic was needed for the common affairs of life. Geometry was of the highest importance for the determination of the limits of the fields after the inundation had withdrawn, carrying with it all the land-marks between the deserts; nor was it of less value for the measurement of materials and all matters connected with the cost of building. For the architects and many of the scribes, mechanics, in which the Egyptians were great, formed a necessary study. Chemistry must have been a branch of learning. Medicine was eagerly studied from the earliest ages; yet the Egyptians were far behind the Mosaic Law in sanitary regulations, in which, indeed, that code has anticipated modern science. Those who would find a career in the great body of official scribes must have learnt the principles and practice of law. It seems strange that philosophy does not seem to have been a regular branch of study. We must recollect that the colleges were under the control of the priests, and that the moralists, the only Egyptian philosophers of the period before the Greek rule, were their natural opponents. The writings of some of the earlier moralists must, however, have been studied as types of classical composition.

To us who are accustomed to the vast range of studies at our universities, this seems a narrow scheme of education; but we must not forget that it contained the germ of all later instruction; and that the old Egyptian universities may be favourably compared with the other ancient seats of learning and with those of the Middle Ages.

Such must have been the teaching at the university of Heliopolis. If we had any doubt that Alexandria succeeded to it, this would disappear when we learnt that at the new university the subjects taught were, poetry corresponding to literature in the older university, mathematics astronomy, and medicine. It was merely the ancient system modified for the Greek population. As the obelisks, the ornaments of the old city, were carried away to beautify the new capital, so the seat of learning was transferred from Heliopolis to Alexandria. The earlier Ptolemies, desirous in all ways to develop the capabilities of Egypt, adopted whatever they thought useful in the civilisation of the country. Can it then be doubted that they strove to maintain and extend the native system of teaching? With a jealous and privileged Greek population at the capital this was done with caution; but we can trace the motive throughout their policy. Thus when the streets of Heliopolis became silent, and the houses of the teachers were empty, another university had grown up in the midst of the busy centre of trade, the wealthy Alexandria, now the second heart of Greek wisdom, the new Athens, destined to a longer intellectual supremacy than the ancient 'Eye of Greece.'

It would be interesting to continue the history of the successive seats of learning down to our own time. Through the centuries we should admire the winning step by step of a sure way up the ladder on the lower rungs of which the Egyptian philosopher could only get a footing. For many ages we should reverence the pursuit of wisdom for her own sake, without desire of worldly gain, in universities open to poor and rich alike. Then we should see the sad change which has cast a deep shadow over modern seats of learning, bringing with it the idea that study is a means to an end, and that end merely success in life. Hence the exclusion of the poor students who crowded to Oxford in the days of the Plantagenets; hence the strain of competition, and the speedy flinging away of the books which have exhausted the brain. The inferior knowledge of the centuries that are gone was better than our higher science, so far as it taught the love of wisdom, and left men thirsting for more learning, not surfeited with 'cram.' Perhaps in a better time our children's children may go back to the ancient way, wherein wisdom was a delight because none thought that she could be bought with money, or that she held in her generous hands the coarse rewards of trade.

Within sight of Heliopolis is the great city of Cairo, Masr, the Mother of the World, where during the Arab ages there flourished the greatest university of the East, the centre of the learning of the Muslim nations, shorn of its glory only in our own days by the rivalry of new-fashioned schools after the European model, like the tawdry palaces which show their unblushing ugliness beside the tender beauty of the Arab mosques. To the Azhar, for so is that mosque called which holds the university, still go afoot from all parts of the world, even from the heart of Africa, poor scholars, to be housed and fed at the cost of the endowment, and to be taught without fee by the most learned men of modern Egypt. The range of instruction may be narrow, but the method is noble, and no one comes away disheartened who has the power to learn. There is little doubt that this is the tradition of the old teaching; and many will ask whether our modern system is likely to have so long a life while it lacks the indispensable principle of vitality.

There is nothing to be said in description of the City of the Sun but that the walls may yet be traced, enclosing an irregular square of about half a mile in the measure of each of its sides. This is about twenty times the area of Lincoln's Inn Fields. Thus the city must have been small; and as the precincts of the sacred buildings take up about half this space, the inhabited part was still less than we think at first. Besides the obelisk, there is one interesting relic in the neighbourhood, a very ancient sycamore, gnarled and crooked with age, the survivor of the gardens of the city. To it clings the tradition that the Holy Family rested beneath its shade when they fled into Egypt. There was indeed a large Hebrew population in the country in those days; and the famous settlement of Onias around the temple built for the worship of his countrymen, was not far from Heliopolis. And near the City of the Sun grew the Judæan balsam-trees, which may have been tended by Hebrew gardeners. The tradition is no more than a legend, yet there is no place in Egypt to which the visit of the Holy Family would be more fit than to the almost deserted seat of learning, when it was already the parent of the great university under whose wide-spreading shadow grew and flourished those Hebrew and Christian schools which had so mighty an influence in the annals of the early Church. Thus Heliopolis then represented that which was passing away, not without hope of that which was to come. The least monumental of all the famous sites of Egypt, without temple or tomb, nor any record but the obelisk, which, splendid as it is, bears a barren official inscription, is yet eloquent of greater things than the solemn pyramids of

Memphis, or the storied temples of Thebes. What these tell is rather of Egypt's history than of the world's, and if of the world's history, only of one time and of one line of thought. The idea that Heliopolis suggests is the true progress of the whole human race; for here was the oldest link in the long chain of the schools of learning. The conqueror has demolished the temple; the city, with the houses of the wise men, has fallen into hopeless ruin, down-trodden by the thoughtless peasant as he drives his plough across the site of which he does not know the name. Yet the name and fame of the City of the Sun charm the stranger as of old, while, standing beside the obelisk, he looks back through the long and stately avenue of the ages that are past, and measures the gain in knowledge that patient scholars have won. He sees that phœnix-like power of renewing her youth which gives all wisdom the deathlessness which is at once a type and a presage of immortality. Forms may change and perish, but the essence which they clothe, and often conceal, knows no change but growth, and when it seems to die, only begins a new and brighter life. Nor can the forsaken form ever cease to speak, voiceless though it be, of life which once dwelt within it, as the corn of wheat in the cast-off husk, the human soul in the dried and vacant mummy. So the obelisk still points to the skies, though it no longer draws down by its golden summit the fire which cleaves the clouds that hide the face of heaven.

CHAPTER X.

PI-BESETH

On the eastern side of the Delta, more than half-way from Memphis to Zoan, lay the great city of Pi-beseth, or Bubastis. Vast mounds now mark the site and preserve the name; deep in their midst lie the shattered fragments of the beautiful temple which Herodotus saw, and to which in his days the Egyptians came annually in vast numbers to keep the greatest festival of the year, the assembly of Bast, the goddess of the place. Here after the Empire had fallen, Shishak set up his throne, and for a short space revived the imperial magnificence of Thebes. A strange figure is this first king of Egypt mentioned by name in Scripture, the enemy of Solomon, the ally of Jeroboam, and the spoiler of Solomon's foolish son,— Shishak, the sovereign of oriental origin known to us as the head of a house of Babylonian or Assyrian lineage, who, despite their foreign names, are yet Egyptian Pharaohs, with a devotion to the religion and the policy of their adopted country.

The days of Shishak, though long before the date of the foundation of Rome, are yet modern in the history of ancient Egypt. He headed the Twenty-second of the long array of Thirty Dynasties which mostly, if not all, ruled in succession. For the first notice of Bubastis we must go back to the Second Dynasty, under which, as Manetho tells us, a great and destructive earthquake here occurred. The origin of the city thus belongs to the primæval period; and this agrees with the great popularity of the local worship. For in Egypt it seems that the chief religious centres are generally of remote antiquity. The site had a twofold importance. Between the Pelusiac, or most eastern branch of the Nile, and the Tanitic, it commanded the land route to Palestine from Memphis, and so became a military post when the state was weak, while it remained a great commercial station. The foundation may have been due to the need of a chief town for the fertile country around, but the position favoured its growth.

The Hebrew Pi-beseth and the Greek Bubastis preserve the sacred name of the place, Pe-Bast, the abode of the great goddess Bast. She is portrayed with the head of a lioness or a cat. The solar goddesses have the heads of those animals whose eyes are luminous in the dark, as the solar gods have the head of the strong-eyed hawk who gazes at the sun. Like all the Egyptian divinities, it is hard to distinguish the characteristics of Bast. The priests held that the leading object of worship of one temple must correspond to those of others. Hence an interchange of attributes of different gods and a loss of identity. But it seems that the essential idea of Bast was that she represented solar heat in two forms, its life-giving and its destructive power. If she was likened by the Greeks to Artemis (Diana), she rather resembled the twin-divinity Apollo.

The charm of the city is not due to that vast antiquity which we fail to imagine, nor to the wild popular festival, which shows us the worst aspect of Egyptian life, but to the rise of the line of Shishak, whose history is associated with that of its favourite seat. The house of the Ramesside kings gradually grew weak, and the power fell into the hands of the Theban high-priests of Amen-ra, who at last put aside a feeble sovereign, and assumed the double crown of Upper and Lower Egypt. Usurpation was naturally followed by anarchy, and a strong hand was needed to restore unity to the divided state. It was then that Shishak rose. Whence he came we do not know. In those days the Delta was full of foreign settlers, of whom many were Shemites. But Shishak, his ancestors, and his descendants are not only strangers: almost all bear names which are either Assyrian or Babylonian. His own appears in Hebrew as a name of the city of Babylon : his father was called Nimrod, a common name with this family. It is easy to trace by what steps the throne was mounted. The grandfather of Shishak intermarried into an Egyptian royal family: his father Nimrod gained a great military office. Shishak himself rose higher, and while almost king secured his position by marrying his son to the daughter of an Egyptian Pharaoh. This is quite natural when we consider the great popularity at this time of all that was Shemite, the Egyptian foreign alliances, and the power of the mercenaries. Yet Dr. Brugsch has woven of these scanty materials the idea of an Assyrian conquest of Egypt. The objection to his view is that the Assyrians were then in a condition of obscure depression. Their First Empire, which carried the arms of Assyria into

Phœnicia, had been utterly shattered by the Babylonians and the Hittites, and the Israelite Empire of Solomon had risen upon its ruins. That powerful and strongly-governed state would have blocked the way to Egypt against the warlike Assyrians, had they then had the power to move, and against the pacific Babylonians. Yet as the family of Shishak were held in great honour in Egypt, it may be that they came of one of the eastern reigning houses; they may have been royal fugitives from Assyria, like the Edomite and Israelite exiles who in Solomon's time took refuge at the Egyptian court. As conquerors they certainly did not come, and Brugsch's idea would be paralleled if we imagined a conquest of Greece by Denmark, because a Danish prince is now king of that country.

The new sovereign Shishak, called in Egyptian Sheshonk, was not of the same pacific temper as the last degenerate heirs of the name of Ramses. Politic and warlike, he bided his time until he could strike for imperial power. So long as Solomon reigned he could only encourage the discontent of the Israelites by sheltering Jeroboam. With the death of Solomon and the accession of the feeble Rehoboam, Jeroboam returned from Egypt with engagements to Shishak. The compact was carried out when Pharaoh broke across the border, captured the cities of Judah, and also the Levite cities of Israel, which were true to the house of David. This inroad of Shishak into Israelite territory is a new fact, which we learn from his own record next to be noticed; it reveals the baseness of Jeroboam the son of Nebat, marked with the distinctive term of opprobrium 'who made Israel to sin.' He disliked the Levites, and had not the courage to make a direct attack upon them; so he called in his Egyptian patron to despoil and lead captive his own brethren. Jerusalem escaped only by the sacrifice of the treasures of the temple and the palace. In one campaign Judah was humbled, and the work of David and Solomon shattered: the great edifices plundered symbolised the ruin of the state, its beauty torn from it by the spoiler.

A vast sculpture on the wall of the great temple of Amen-ra at El-Karnak is the triumphal record at Thebes of Shishak's success. With the dimensions of the like works of the Empire, this long list of conquests is by their side insignificant. Instead of countries and nations we find cities and tribes, and even the same name repeated, to tell the subjugation of another family of nomads whom the older Pharaohs would scarcely have mentioned. Yet the details are intensely historical. Here we first read in a foreign document the names of the cities of Israel and Judah in the days of their kings. Unhappily it is a mere list, not a chronicle like the annals of Thothmes and those of the Assyrian kings. The conqueror's list enumerates Levitical and probably Canaanite cities of the kingdom of Israel, cities of the kingdom of Judah, and Arab tribes of the south of Palestine. We recognise at once Taanach, Shunem, Rehob, Haphraim, Adoraim, Mahanaim, Gibeon, Beth-horon, Kedemoth, Aijalon, Megiddo, Ibleam, Shoco, Beth-tappuah, the Hagarites and the district of Negeb, the one occurring seven times, the other three, quite contrary to the usual practice in the tables of conquests. Early in the list, following a group of cities of Israel, comes the strange name Iudah Malek, followed by the determinative sign which distinguishes foreign countries. This name consists of two words, in appearance the Hebrew 'Judah king,' which gave rise to the notion that Rehoboam himself, the king of Judah, was intended. This, however, could not be, for the contents of these lists are always geographical. If the meaning is kingdom of Judah, the words are inverted, and the second misspelt. If we divide the words differently as Iuda Hamelek, they would read 'Judah the king,' but we know of no town of that name. For the present we must be content with having read the name of Judah in the list, leaving it to time to decide whether the kingdom or a city was intended.

The splendour of the reign of Shishak was not maintained by his successors. It may have been followed by a foreign invasion, for Zerah the Ethiopian, defeated by Asa (2 Chron. xiv. 9-15), was possibly a priest-king of Napata, and if so, he must have subdued Egypt for a time, like later sovereigns of the same line. We soon find the Bubastite king a feeble central authority, the shadow of a departed power, nominally ruling a number of small chiefs, who were in fact independent. This was due to a fatal custom of the Bubastites, who divided their territories among princes of their family, by whose side Egyptians and Libyans ultimately rose to the same rank; and thus, less than two centuries after the reign of Shishak, Egypt was separated into about twenty petty kingdoms without a head. The country was not so much broken into fragments as resolved into its primitive elements, the nomes, or provinces. Each nome had retained its individual worship and customs, and was still a little state, in spite of the ages of strong central rule, and the moments of violent conquest. The central power withdrawn or enfeebled, the nomes asserted their natural independence. The house of Shishak was not extinct, for among the little chiefs it had its representatives, who still ruled as late as the time of the great conflict between the mighty powers of Assyria and Ethiopia, when the divided princes served as tools of the diplomatic antagonists, both of whom they disliked, and striving to baffle only served. Thus all disappeared but the one patriotic line, that of Saïs, which overthrew its rivals, and for nearly a century and a half restored Egypt to a greatness she had not known since the reign of Shishak.

Little can now be seen of the ancient splendour of Bubastis. The lofty mounds rise above the level of the temple, for the city grew, as the people of each period built on the ruins of the fragile houses of their ancestors, while the sacred precincts remained on their first site. The old Egyptians were careful builders. In the Delta, where they had not the dry desert for a foundation, and the Nile moisture would destroy ordinary stone, they used the most enduring material, the red granite of Syene, and the columns, instead of being of several blocks, were solid monoliths. The great temple at Iseum, northward of Bubastis, was wholly built of this splendid substance. The lavish cost of transporting from the extreme south of Egypt these vast blocks, and covering them with finely-cut sculptures, is far beyond our power of estimate. We cannot realise what such labour would be, aided by none but the simplest mechanical appliances, nor the difficulty of delicately engraving every part of the masses with a sureness of hand that is amazing.

Like all the other temples of the Delta, those of Bubastis have fallen to the ground. This universal ruin may be partly due to the rage of invaders, whose force may be was almost spent when they reached Upper Egypt, for there we see far less destruction. Yet it is hard to account for the overthrow of all the sumptuous edifices of the Delta, constructed of far stronger materials than their southern rivals. The great temple of Iseum, for instance was in its bulk a Ptolemaic work, and thus mainly of an age after the destructive invasions. It seems to have been overthrown by an earthquake, for it has fallen like a house of cards. Yet there is no record of earthquakes in Egypt violent enough to hurl down such solid walls and columns, put together on the simplest constructive principles, and so forming a mass, strong both in independent members, and as a whole. The slender Arab minarets have suffered from such shocks, but to no great extent, in spite of their comparative weakness, and the neglect in recent centuries to take the simplest measures for their preservation.

At Bubastis there are remains of two temples, that of the goddess Bast and of Hermes (Mercury), by whom we suppose Herodotus must mean the Egyptian god of letters, Thoth. They show large use of granite, with the usual columns in a single block. Excavation here would yield interesting results. There is much obscurity in the annals of the house of Shishak : this surely would be cleared up. Earlier and later records would be certain to afford pages of history, perhaps from the very oldest period of the monarchy, for king after king would have contributed to the great temple of the goddess. If Thoth were here especially worshipped, there must have been a college of learned men at the place, and the very potsherds would give us the exercises of the pupils, for such we remember were the slates on which they wrote their copies of classical models of style.

Herodotus speaks of the annual festival of the goddess as the greatest in Egypt, bringing vast numbers of people here to a scene of wild revelry. Though the hamlet that recalls the name of the old town has ceased to be a place of resort, we may almost say that the festival survives, and has been transferred to Tanta, in the centre of the Delta, and is held in honour of a Muslim saint, Seyyid Ahmad El-Bedawee. No one could have been more averse than Mohammad to heathen customs, most of all to those which were associated with religion, yet he has been everywhere defeated by the human tendency to cling to ancient superstitions and time-honoured usages. So in Christian countries pagan customs have survived. Thus a new saint, Muslim or Christian, becomes the centre of the old reverence; the name is changed, but the surroundings are the same. At an Arab saint's tomb in Upper Egypt a sacred snake is still, or lately was, revered; the predecessors of the reptile were no doubt put under the protection of a Coptic saint, to whose shrine the ancient Egyptian worship had been in turn transferred. Thus the Delta still witnesses one great annual festival, at which under the name of religion a fair is kept, with the accompaniments of the heathen meeting to which the pilgrims in the days of Herodotus resorted. A few go to join in religious services in honour of the saint—services, be it remarked, of a kind which Mohammad disliked for their connection with monasticism, the wild zikrs of the darweeshes; but the many go to take their pleasure in witnessing the spectacle of the dancing-girls, who are the true descendants of the old Egyptian dancers, and in all kinds of revelry, such as scandalised Herodotus.

The memory of the lower elements of the Egyptian religion is nowhere stronger than here at Bubastis. No such idea is suggested by the great necropolis of Memphis, with the symbols of immortality in the vast Pyramids, and that absence of figures of the gods in the ancient tombs around them, which has led those who cannot read the inscriptions to believe that they are in the presence of records of a simple faith such as was that of the few high-souled philosophers of that remote age. At Thebes, though the temples are full of the idolatry of the Empire, in the royal tombs we trace an attempt to see in that confusion the many developments of one great power. But at Bubastis there is nothing to be traced but the debasing animal worship suggesting the orgies that accompanied it. The golden calf and the wild dancing multitude rise before our eyes, and we feel with full force the need of those stern prohibitions in which the Law and the Prophets abound. It is a relief to turn to the tale of the house of Shishak, the rise in Africa of a strong Asiatic power and its speedy withering away, the first interference of Egypt in the politics of Israel, and the new light thrown on the conflict of the two little Hebrew kingdoms which were the surviving fragments of the great Empire of Solomon, vanished for ever, to be the regretful retrospect of history and the subject of golden legends. So many and so various are the thoughts which rise at this one site, a mere heap of mounds, strewn in their hollow with the shattered fragments of the temples of Bubastis. Below the surface lie the lost books of history, to be taken up and read by whoso will. Egypt, the land of history, hides in every mound the imperishable records of the past. To the present belongs the rich inheritance, waiting like a land of promise for the heir, who has only to go in and take possession of this stored-up wealth. Difficulties and dangers there are none to be encountered. The treasure-houses are unguarded by mighty men, no mountains have to be passed on the way. The very ease of the enterprise has discouraged those who have mettle to scale the towering Alps and seek the North Pole across its barriers of icy desert. Yet the reward is far greater than the mere sense of achievement which the other enterprises offer. The story of the oldest civilisations, the far-reaching tradition of science and art, the wanting links in the histories of ancient nations, Egyptians, Chaldæans, Assyrians, Hebrews, and Greeks, such are the buried treasures of these neglected mounds. At the touch of the pick the people of the past rise like the mighty army of bones which the prophet saw, are clothed again with flesh, and march in their ranks along the ancient lines of primæval history. It is for us to awake them from their long sleep.

On the wild coast of Cornwall, where the black craggy height of Tintagel faces the stormy Atlantic, there lingers yet, coming and going, like a fitful breeze, the legend of Arthur. Here he held his court. At Slaughter

Bridge, a few miles inland, in his last battle he faced the traitor Modred and the heathen host. So far may be history, but the passing of the king and the casting of Excalibur into such a mere as may be seen from the heights of the granite-capped mountains, these are mere fancies, delighting the imagination but baffling the desire for true records. In Egypt all is pure history. Each fresh discovery rescues the subjects of legend from its misty realm. Within the memory of living men, the great figures of Egyptian antiquity were such shadowy types as Sesostris, a mere embodiment of a series of conquerors, but knowledge of the monuments has given us the living materials out of which this Colossus of legend was built. So too it is with the vagueness which inevitably surrounds the early Pharaohs of Bible history, whose names and dates are unrecorded. As each is identified, with his great works and wise politics, it is as if the pick of some Cornish labouring man were to strike upon a tablet of King Arthur, in fair Latin, dated, and with all historic circumstance. Such a thought makes us feel it were wise to wake from dreaming of legends, and to arise to explore the sure ways of history.

CHAPTER XI.

SIN.

THE approaches to Egypt give no promise of the beauty of the land within, which, like such an oasis as the plain of Damascus, fills the eye with fresh delight. From the south you thread the narrow passage between the tumbled rocks of the Cataract, while all around rise masses of sterile granite, the more forbidding because the restful charm of Philæ is fresh in your memory; from the west you cross the monotonous Libyan desert by the dreary coast; from the east you only leave the quicksands of Lake Serbonis behind to enter a wide-extending morass of dark-brown mud. Should you come by sea, the stretch of low sandy shore is only less uninviting than the desert routes. But the long and weary way of which Homer speaks is now most true of the journey from the east, which despite its historical interest few care to undertake. On this side the Delta pushes a sharp angle into the desert. Behind, as we enter Egypt, is the treacherous Lake Serbonis; in front, the great marsh broadening towards the west; on the right, the level melancholy shore of the almost tideless Mediterranean. At the very point of the angle stood of old the great stronghold Pelusium, Sin, in Ezekiel's days, 'the strength of Egypt' (xxx. 15). The most eastward Nile-stream flowed behind the city, and on the north was a port commodious enough to hold an ancient fleet. There was no other harbour along the inhospitable and dangerous coast, though, where Alexandria afterwards arose, Greek ships had already found a shelter when unable to enter the branch of the Nile which led to their emporium Naucratis. Thus Pelusium was the key of Egypt, whether the invader came by sea or by land.

The foundation of the stronghold is obscure. In the days of the Empire, the Pharaohs, mindful of the conquest of their country by the Shepherds, covered the east of the Delta with fortresses. As they were the first kings who maintained a fleet in the Mediterranean, the harbour of Pelusium was probably constructed by them, and we may reasonably date the importance of the city from that time, though Zoan, more pleasantly placed amid well-watered meadow-lands, was then the great emporium of the border. It may be that Pelusium was far more ancient. Except Memphis we do not know the date of the foundation of a single Egyptian town of importance; there are no young cities in that old country; even Alexandria grew round and swallowed up the more ancient Rhakotis. It seems as if Egypt were so populous in the very beginning of her history that almost every good site was held -before the written records were graven for our instruction.

The Hebrew name Sin, like the Greek Pelusium, means 'muddy,' and is retained in the Arab 'Castle of Teeneh,' an outlying fort. If Dr. Brugsch's conjecture is right, the Egyptians called the city Ha-snetem, 'the abode of sweet repose.' The Shemites thought of the weary waste of morass which here met their eyes, the Egyptians of the delight of resting safely in the first native town across the border. Lying, as the city did, in the Shemite part of Egypt, the local worship under the Empire was, like that of Zoan, a mixture of the Egyptian and the Shepherd systems, according to the policy of the Ramesside kings.

As the Egyptian monarchy waned, Pelusium grew in

importance, for it was the strongest city of the border. Here the last king of the Saïte line, Psammetichus III., son of Amasis, awaited Cambyses. The battle of Pelusium, which crushed the native power, may almost take rank among the decisive battles of the world. Had the Persians failed, they might never have won the command of the Mediterranean, without which they could scarcely have invaded Greece. Of the details of the action we know nothing. The Egyptians were probably far outnumbered, and the native soldiery disheartened by the presence of Greek and Carian mercenaries, by whose side they never fought their best. Yet it was a stubborn conflict, but at last the Egyptian army gave way and fled in rout to Memphis. Herodotus, some seventy years afterwards, visited the battle-field, and saw the bones of the Egyptians and the Persians still strewn upon the ground, apart from one another as they had fallen. Thus, the Egyptians must have long held their own, and been slain in their ranks, rather than in their flight.

Egypt never recovered from this blow. True, throughout the Persian rule there were patriotic revolts, and the land had moments of independence, but it was not until the great Eastern empire was far gone in decay that a native ruler at last expelled the stranger. Yet the Persians under Artaxerxes Ochus once more invaded Egypt, and again an Egyptian king, Nectanabis, awaited them before Pelusium. Every preparation had been made for a stout defence. But no great battle was fought. On each side the best troops were Greek mercenaries, and those in the Persian pay outmanœuvred their rivals. The position of Nectanabis was turned, and he fled to Memphis, and without waiting the fortune of war, gathered his treasures and disappeared into Ethiopia. From that day to this no native prince has sat upon the throne of Egypt. (Comp. Ezek. xxx. 12, 13; Zech. x. 11.)

Three centuries pass by, Egypt has welcomed Alexander as her deliverer from the Persian yoke, the great city Alexandria has been founded and has put Pelusium into the shade, Greek kings have ruled Egypt, and their mighty and prosperous empire has dwindled into a distracted kingdom, living only by favour of Rome. Young Ptolemy, fourteenth of his name, who occupies the throne, is a minor governed by unscrupulous ministers. One day a Roman fleet of galleys and transports, with two thousand soldiers on board, appears before

Pelusium. Pompey, defeated at Pharsalia, has come with the remnants of his showy army to beg an asylum from Ptolemy, whose father was secured by him on the throne. At this moment Ptolemy and his sister, the famous Cleopatra, are at war, and their armies lie near Pelusium. The fugitive general at once sends a message to the king. The ministers see that the force of Pompey would determine the present conflict, but they fear Cæsar, and so resolve to get rid of the dangerous visitor. A little boat is sent to Pompey's galley, and he enters it with a few attendants. The king stands with his courtiers waiting by the seaside. At this moment the Egyptian galleys are manned by armed men, and troops are ranged along the shore. As Pompey rises to step on land he is stabbed in the back by an infamous Roman, once an officer of his own, now in the Egyptian service. He draws his toga over his face with both hands, and falls. Cornelia, his faithful wife, and his friends, watching from his galley, see the deed in helpless horror. The assassins carry away Pompey's head, leaving his naked body on the beach. The Roman fleet sails away. A faithful freedman Philippus, who had come ashore in the boat with his master, washes the dead with sea-water, and raises a little funeral pyre of the fragments of an old fishing-craft. Afterwards, the Egyptian army having disappeared, the ashes were collected and taken to the sad widow, who piously deposited them in her husband's villa near Alba. Cæsar in hot pursuit soon reached Egypt. The murderers offered him as a welcome present the head and the signet-ring of Pompey. He turned away in tears, and commanded the miscreants to be put to death. Then he raised a monument to his rival's memory at the place where he was slain. It was visited in later times, but its site is now lost in the sandy coast. Three months after the treachery at Pelusium, the young king of Egypt was drowned.

The scene of Pompey's death is not less striking than that of Cæsar's. The melancholy shore, crowded with Alexandrian Greeks and Egyptians around the puppet young king and his sinister advisers, the army of many races and various accoutrements, the great Captain falling with the gesture with which Cæsar was soon to fall, struck like Cæsar by the treachery of a friend, the dark blue sea in which the huge galleys lie reflected, with high poops and with indented beaks, while on the deck of one near to the shore may be seen the grief-stricken Cornelia, and Pompey's comrades—all this seems to rise before us in the bright sunshine of an Egyptian September, for it befell on the twenty-ninth of that month, the day before Pompey's birthday, in the year B.C. 48. The dignity of Roman character, not yet lost, elevates the event to the height of a tragedy, fitly closing with the brave fidelity of the freedman and the tenderness and respect of the rival leader.

The battlefield of Pelusium, the entrenchments of Nectanabis, the tomb of Pompey, all have vanished, and nothing now remains of the great stronghold but mighty mounds with an outlying height of the same kind near by, and a second farther away, rising from the level of the dreary marsh, close to the seashore. It is an awful desolation, wearying the eye with an unvaried dark expanse, without a sign of life, and wearying the feet with the treacherous soil, in which they sink deeper and deeper on the way to Pelusium. And the air seems heavy with sad memories, as if they were native to the place.[1]

---

[1] The latest and best description of Pelusium and the neighbouring sites is in Mr. Greville Chester's Report (Quarterly Statement of Palestine Exploration Fund, July 1880, p. 133, foll.)

Pelusium has an historical lesson to tell, which explains the two great catastrophes her name recalls. The two Persian invasions were successful at once because the Egyptian kings staked all on the strength of the eastern border. They thought that Pelusium and the neighbouring forts were support enough for an army of defence. This army defeated or outflanked, the whole of Lower Egypt was at once open to the invader. Yet the story of the war of independence, which almost filled the time between the invasions, shows that Egypt could be obstinately defended step by step. In fact it is a country like Holland. The whole water-system, natural and artificial, lends itself to military engineering, and during the inundation it could be used with tremendous effect. Psammetichus and Nectanabis failed because they feared to lose the power of retreating to Memphis, and from Memphis to Thebes and Ethiopia. The same has been the case in other periods of Egyptian history : a single battle has decided the fate of the country. Scarcely at any time but during the patriotic rise against the Persians has the defensive power of nature been wisely used.

Both Jeremiah and Ezekiel speak of another great

frontier-town, variously written Tahpanhes, Tehaphnehes, Tahaphanes, which has been identified with Daphnæ, which Herodotus calls the Pelusiac Daphnæ, sixteen Roman miles south-westward of Pelusium. The Hebrew name is evidently of Egyptian origin. It also occurs in the form Tahpenes as that of a queen who was probably consort of Shishak's predecessor (1 Kings xi. 19, 20). She is the only Egyptian queen, and the first Egyptian royal personage, who is mentioned by name in the Bible. The identity of the name of queen and town would not be proof of Egyptian origin, for Semitic names were then the rule in the foreign family of Shishak, and in fashion with the natives. It is the uncertainty of the orthography which shows that the source is not Hebrew. The Greek name compared with it is clearly an adaptation, and until we know more from Egyptian sources we cannot be sure that Daphnæ was identical with the town mentioned in the Bible. The evidence is, however, far better than a mere likeness in sound. Clearly Tahpanhes was a great military settlement (Jer. ii. 16), and a frontier-fortress (Ezek. xxx. 18), where Pharaoh had a palace (Jer. xliii. 9). The position on the border is farther defined if we assume that this was the point first reached by the Jews in their flight after the murder of **Gedaliah** (ver. 7), and the place may be even more clearly fixed as between Migdol and Memphis (xliv. 1). **Herodotus** speaks of the Pelusiac Daphnæ as one of the three great garrison-towns of Egypt, in the south, east, and west, under the very kings in whose time the prophets lived (ii. 30).

The site of Daphnæ is supposed to be marked by the lofty mounds of Tel-Defneh, occupying a position which would agree with the evidence of geography, but no remains of importance are seen above the ground. There could be no better post to hold as a central position on the frontier and as a support to Pelusium.

The disappearance from history of the towns of the eastern border was due to the foundation of Alexandria, and to the naval power of the Ptolemies. The capital was thus removed far beyond the risk of sudden attack, and could always be provisioned by sea, nor could an invader venture to march on Memphis and the Upper Country, while Alexandria remained unsubdued. Thus for centuries the eastern fortresses lost their importance, and the towns they enclosed or protected dwindled and disappeared, until the transfer of the capital to the Arab cities near Memphis, of which Cairo is the latest, made it necessary to strengthen the border once more. The researches of Brugsch have restored the old cities to the map, but they are merely known as shapeless heaps untouched by the explorer. A little labour in these mounds would settle many a curious question that we dispute about in vain. A single inscribed fragment would reveal the Egyptian name of Daphnæ, and settle the question whether it was identical with the city to which Jeremiah came and predicted the very spot where the king of Babylon should spread his royal tent and set up his throne before Pharaoh's house (Jer. xliii. 8-10).

CHAPTER XII.

ALEXANDRIA.

ALEXANDRIA, the city of Alexander, is his best monument. His two leading ideas, the extension of commerce and the fusion of the Greeks and the Orientals, led him to choose the site of the city and to frame the constitution. It is equally characteristic of him that Homer guided him to the place. Few men can travel without favourite books, the companions by whom they may be known. Alexander carried with him Homer. The famous copy 'of the casket' took its name from the case for unguents captured in the treasure of Darius, in which the victor put the most precious work of man's mind in the costliest work of his hand. Thenceforward the casket lay, with a dagger, beneath Alexander's pillow wherever he went. Can we doubt that he knew the passage in the Odyssey where the poet describes the one sheltered roadstead of the northern coast of Egypt, the harbour behind the island of Pharos, a day's voyage for a ship sped with a fair wind from the nearest mouth of the Nile?

> Upon the surging ocean wave there lies a rocky isle,
> 'Tis Pharos called, which stands against the opening of the Nile,
> So far as in a single day a hollow ship may fare,
> If on her sheet the whistling wind shall favourably bear.
> Behind the island is a port where galleys ride secure,
> Until, their watery load baled out, they venture forth once more.

Here the old Greek merchantmen must have taken shelter till they could run in fine weather for the river and cross the bar to ascend to their emporium, Naucratis. If Alexander had come to Egypt on a voyage of discovery, he would have surveyed the whole coast. Instead of this, he marches from Pelusium to Memphis, and from Memphis makes almost direct for the site of Alexandria on his way to the oracle of Jupiter Ammon.

When Alexander reached the Egyptian military station at the little town or village of Rhakotis, he saw with the quick eye of a great commander how to turn this petty settlement into a great city, and to make its roadstead, out of which ships could be blown by a change of wind, into a double harbour roomy enough to shelter the navies of the world. All that was needed was to join the island by a mole to the continent. The site was admirably secure and convenient, a narrow strip of land between the Mediterranean and the great inland Lake Mareotis. The whole northern side faced the two harbours, which were bounded east and west by the mole, and beyond by the long narrow rocky island of Pharos, stretching parallel with the coast. On the south was the inland port of Lake Mareotis. The length of the city was more than three miles, the breadth more than three-quarters of a mile; the mole was above three-quarters of a mile long and six hundred feet broad; its breadth is now doubled, owing to the silting up of the sand. Modern Alexandria until lately only occupied the mole, and was a great town in a corner of the space which Alexander, with large provision for the future, measured out. The form of the new city was ruled by hat of the site, but the fancy of Alexander designed it in the shape of a Macedonian cloak or chlamys, such as a national hero wears on the coins of the kings of Macedon, his ancestors.

The situation is excellent for commerce. Alexandria, with the best Egyptian harbour on the Mediterranean, and the inland port connected with the Nile-streams and canals, was the natural emporium of the Indian trade. Port Said is superior now because of its grand artificial port, and the advantage for steamships of an unbroken sea-route. But in earlier days it was better to diminish the length of the Indian voyage through the dangerous route of the Red Sea, and so the Ptolemies favoured the higher ports on the eastern coast, connected by roads with the Nile in the Thebaïs. No position in Egypt is so good for defence as that of Alexandria. The narrow strip of land, washed by the water on the north and south, was only open to the east and west. The east alone was the side by which a formidable enemy would approach; on the other side there were only the roving tribes of Libyans. There were two drawbacks, the difficulty of entering the double harbour on account of the reefs which barred it, and the want of water. Yet the harbour was the best on the coast, and a splendid lighthouse, called the Pharos, on the eastern point of the island, lessened the dangers of the ships. A canal conducted fresh water to the city by the western or less assailable side, and cisterns were cut in the rock to store the rain. The practical wisdom of the choice for trade and security was amply justified by history. Alexandria was for ages the pivot of the Indian traffic, and so long as invasion was attempted by land, before the days of great naval expeditions, Egypt could not be subdued as easily as before. It were useless to march on Memphis while the capital remained untouched in the rear of the enemy and could draw supplies of men and munitions from the sea, for the Ptolemies maintained a fleet, and Cyprus was to them a place of arms.

The interest of Alexandria is not so much political as literary, yet a few words must be said of her place in history during the nine centuries and a half of her greatness. To tell the story in detail would be to relate that of Egypt. The capital of the Ptolemies, and till near the time of the Arab conquest the seat of the Roman governor, the one great centre of Greek life, was the very heart of whatever lands she ruled. Here Ptolemy fixed his seat of government, and he or his successor with great solemnity brought the body of Alexander in a golden coffin to rest in the city he had named. Here he began to carry out the great schemes which Alexander only lived long enough to plan. The Pharos was then built to light the way into the harbour. The palace, the arsenal, the docks, the temple of Sarapis, then rose from the ground; it may be that the old king witnessed the foundation of the Library and the Museum. But the magnificence of the capital was due to his son, the wealthiest of ancient kings, Ptolemy, surnamed Philadelphus. During a long and peaceful reign he and his consort, the second Arsinoë, laboured to fill the city with noble edifices and with the science and learning of Greece. The Museum was crowded with teachers and students, the Library with eager readers, the streets were thronged with the crowds of traffickers, and with the idlers who flocked to the great pageants of the king and the scenes of the theatre. The picture of a royal pomp, as given by Callixenus with heraldic precision, that of the life of the rich ladies, as drawn by Theocritus with poetic liveliness, are not so striking as the little story how the rich and luxurious king looked from his palace-window, and as he saw the naked children sporting on the sand, cried 'Would that I were one of them!' It is the old summing up of Solomon,— 'Vanity of vanities, all is vanity!'

The successor of Philadelphus, Ptolemy surnamed Euergetes, the Benefactor, is the first king who while still a Greek began to be an Egyptian also. A quarrel with the Syrian ruler, for the sake of his sister, murdered by a rival queen, led Euergetes to make war on his eastern neighbour. In a splendid campaign he revived the fame of the ancient Pharaohs, and the people of Egypt rejoiced when he brought back to the shrines the statues which the Persians had carried away. Berenice, beautiful and virtuous, shared his throne, and the court and city of Alexandria then reached their highest prosperity. The first century of the city's life now closed, and the decline began. Weak kings could not govern well at home, nor abroad make head against their turbulent neighbours of Syria. Pretenders in their own family took advantage of the difficulties of the heads of the house. Very soon Rome began to protect, to interfere, and to weaken, and it was only under the splendid reign of Cleopatra, ambitious, unscrupulous, but yet the last brilliant heir of Alexander's genius, that Egypt for a while recovered her greatness. Then came the catastrophe, and the Roman Empire gained a rich and turbulent province; for under the later kings a new force appeared in Egyptian politics, the restless Greek populace of Alexandria. Strong enough to expel a tyrant, they had lost the Hellenic sense of liberty, and only called in a fresh tyrant in his stead. Their part was not a noble one. They were more and more isolated from the rest of Egypt. The efforts of patriots to establish a native dynasty found no sympathy with the Alexandrians. The momentary independence of Thebes, and later the noble struggle in which the ancient capital perished, were witnessed with indifference, if not with aversion. The Alexandrian mob had sunk into a chaos of unrest where they blindly wandered, with no purpose but the desire of the moment for pleasure or for revenge.

Yet this mob ruled Egypt under the weaker of the Greek kings and Roman governors. The whole administration was centralised at Alexandria, and the pressure of popular clamour could move the machine of the state when it was uncontrolled by a master's hand. Thus in time the centre ceased to have any influence but that of brute force on the rest of Egypt. In the later days of the Roman rule this restless population was drawn into the religious conflicts which made the country an easy prey to the Arabs—but this belongs to a later part of the subject.

One would curiously inquire whether Alexander planned all that his city became under the Ptolemies, his successors in the Egyptian part of his great empire. He had thought of a commercial centre, and had designed for it a constitution which should unite, after his favourite policy, the Greek and the Egyptian in a common citizenship. The Ptolemies maintained the interests of trade. They varied the constitution by introducing Hebrew citizens on a level with the Greeks, while they gave the Egyptians an inferior place, thus injuring the scheme in the very direction in which they enlarged it. To their action, though the idea may have been Alexander's, it was due that their capital became a second Athens, the centre of the Greek world, the meeting-place of the intelligence of the East and the West in a nobler commerce than that which filled the docks and the markets with the merchandise of every sea which Greek and Phœnician galleys traversed, of every land into which caravans could penetrate. The Museum and the Library of Alexandria have outshone the fame of her luxury and trade. When her name is mentioned, we think not of a stately city, but of the long roll of patient students who there led the schools of thought which we call Alexandrian, of the hardy pioneers of science, and of our large debt to those early labourers who toiled for our profit; and we remember that greatest ancient treasure of books, the loss of which we ceaselessly deplore, for most of them are known to us only by name or from a tantalising fragment.

The intellectual activity of Alexandria was centred in the Museum and the Library, but we cannot understand these institutions unless we look at the whole atmosphere of thought in which they grew up. We have not only to trace the origin of a great school of philosophy, the parent of other schools, and to observe a series of momentous movements in the early Church; we must not neglect the history of a new belief which was destined to take a leading part in the final conflict of paganism and Christianity.

The mixed Greek and Egyptian population of Alexandria needed a religion such as a centre of learning could not give them. The introduction of the worn-out creed of Egypt would have been distasteful to the Greeks, a foreign worship would have met little favour with the Egyptians. Accordingly the astute old king who founded the Ptolemaic dynasty solved the difficulty by the ingenious compromise which introduced an Egyptian belief in a Hellenic form. On the pretext of a dream he despatched messengers to Sinope on the Euxine, for a sacred statue; on its arrival he consulted the Egyptian priests, and they pronounced it to represent Sarapis, a form of Osiris, the ruler of the world of shades, supposed to be embodied in Apis, the living sacred bull of Memphis. Thus the worship of Osiris, the most human phase of the native religion, became the popular faith of the capital. The animal worship was suppressed at Alexandria, but its relation to the Alexandrian divinity readily introduced the new ideas at Memphis, where the Egyptian Sarapis was already reverenced. This new belief, touching as it did the hopes and fears of mankind, speedily gained a wide popularity. It spread throughout Egypt, and thence to the dominions of the Ptolemies on the southern shore of Asia Minor. It crossed the Ægean to Greece, and the Adriatic to Rome. Yet it was but a popular creed. The learned men of Alexandria treated it with indifference, if not with contempt, until at length they sought its aid in the final conflict with Christianity.

The Alexandrian schools of philosophy grew in and around the Museum and the Library; of these we must learn something if we would understand what they produced.

The first two Ptolemies, who for nearly eighty years ruled the richest and most tranquil part of the Empire of Alexander, had nothing more at heart than the welfare of their capital. Their policy was so completely one that we do not know to which of the two we should assign the twin foundations which are the true glory of the city, because they made it for at least seven centuries the mainspring of the intellectual movement of the civilised world. Like the Mausoleum of Halicarnassus, and the Pharos of Alexandria, the Museum has given its name to a whole class of successors. But it was not a treasury of statues and pictures; the masterpieces of art were at that time enshrined in temples and palaces. True to its name, the Temple of the Muses was a university, yet it contained in its precincts some of the elements of an ideal museum, and thus the large scope of its plan hints that a museum should be a university, and that a university cannot be complete without collections, an unconscious satire on the modern divorce of two institutions most necessary to each other's life.

Nothing in Greece was the pattern of the Museum of Alexandria. Although the Athenian youth had a regular training, the idea of a centre not alone for instruction, but also, it may be rather, for the prosecution of research, was new to the Greeks. They owed it to the Egyptians, and the very system of Heliopolis was carried on at Alexandria. At each city the university was attached to a temple, at each there was a regular staff of professors who at once taught and studied, at each the scope of the subjects had a general similarity.

We know much of the learned men of the Museum; of the establishment itself we know but little. Thus much is certain: there were four faculties, as we should call them, poetry, mathematics, astronomy, and medicine. A botanical garden, which became a garden of acclimatisation, was attached to the Museum, as well as a menagerie; and thus natural history, partly as an aid to medicine, partly for its own sake, had a place in the teaching. Surprising as it seems, philosophy was left out. It was the policy of the Ptolemies to avoid studies which could cast doubt on the moral basis of their system of government, and overthrow the religion of Egypt, with its new development, the worship of Sarapis. Even the priest of the Museum might have lost his influence. He was an important functionary, who stood at the head of the establishment like the rector of a modern college. Next him were the professors. They were the most learned men of the time, attracted by the dignity, the influence, and the emoluments of their offices. For they were salaried by the state. The buildings comprised a great dining-hall, which was the common room of the professors, their theatre for public disputations, their columned corridor for peripatetic lectures, and their private apartments.

It is so usual to speak of the Library of Alexandria, that we need to be reminded that it was twofold. The Library proper was attached to the Museum, but a second great collection was housed, probably for want of room, far away in the Temple of Sarapis. Of the extent of the collections as a whole various accounts are given, perhaps owing to the usual confusion between books and volumes, perhaps with reference to different times. One estimate is 500,000 volumes; and it is said that the library of the Temple of Sarapis was by a single addition augmented to the extent of 200,000 volumes, when the collection of the kings of Pergamus was given by Mark Antony to Cleopatra. If we take a low estimate, a library wholly of manuscripts would not have been insignificant beside its greatest modern successors of the earlier half of this century, though in these recent libraries manuscripts are but a small item beside the vast array of printed books. But number is no test of value. That which sharpens our regret is the quality of the books, of which the loss has cost the life's labour of generations of scholars, striving day and night to work back corrupt texts into the purity in which the Alexandrian Library possessed them, or hopelessly studying a broken fragment of a book which was there complete.

There was a time of repose before the vast material of the Library was brought to bear on speculative thought. The limits of teaching at the Museum, and the predominance of the practical side of knowledge, made the Alexandrian learning at first sceptical and critical. As sceptical it did not attach itself to any one of the great schools of thought. As critical it devoted itself to the heavy work of examining, comparing, and revising the vast body of Greek literature now for the first time brought together. The poets especially were eagerly studied, and we owe our text of Homer to the careful labour of the learned men of Alexandria. Thus the earliest school of Alexandria was eminently practical. In the sphere of imagination it produced nothing. The Alexandrian poetry is sometimes exotic, like the Idylls of Theocritus, but is generally a copy more or less tasteful of old masters. Original art was of necessity absent. There is no style of Alexandria at the very time when Pergamus and Rhodes were showing great originality and mastery of form. When the Greeks at Alexandria returned to the poetry and imagination of philosophy, art, which cannot live without a perpetual tradition, could no longer be revived.

The first traces of a definite school of philosophy at Alexandria are seen where we should least expect them. In an Egyptian temple of the Ptolemaic age, when we are given the key which the genius of Mariette discovered, we find ourselves in the presence of national ideas transformed by Greek influence. The very art has received a new impulse, and the graces of Greek architecture, dead at Alexandria, live again in the Thebaïs under an Egyptian shape. The system of the different parts of the edifice is changed from the mere chance of older times to a strict method. Each hall and chamber has its proper purpose, its suitable sculptures and inscriptions, leading up from the lower stages of knowledge to initiation into the higher truths. At the end of the temple, in the sanctuary, the king worships the Ideas of Plato's philosophy, the Beautiful, the True, and the Good.

Yet this transfusion of new life into the long dead

belief of Egypt was fatal in its effect. A religion which had fallen into helpless decay could only disappear at the touch of philosophy. Thus at the moment when all its greatest thoughts were clothed in worthy form, a deep and hopeless doubt seized on the minds of the people, except those few who could accept the new view without losing whatever was worth retaining in the old doctrines. It was through them that the Alexandrian thinkers received a current of Egyptian influence.

Still more remarkable was the meeting' of Greek and Hebrew thought, and the share which Plato took in their fusion. The Jews of Alexandria, dwelling in a Greek city and speaking its language, soon needed a translation of the Law into their vulgar tongue. Tradition says that this important work was executed by the desire of the second Ptolemy, but it is more reasonable to think that it was due to the care of the Alexandrian sanhedrim. From that moment the logic and philosophy of Greece gave a more fixed form to Hebrew thought, and suggested its definition; from that moment the Platonists were offered that which they had long desired, the reality of their great leader's noble Ideas. A whole literature of the Alexandrian Hebrews attested their largeness of mind and their knowledge of Greek philosophy. In our much-neglected Apocrypha, the Wisdom of Solomon is a splendid instance of this new direction of thought. But the most remarkable productions of this school are the writings of Philo, the earliest Platonist of Alexandria. Philo is indeed the great thinker of the age, in whom we first see the mighty effect of the translation of the Hebrew Scriptures into Greek. He has found the philosophic grammar by which to arrange the thoughts of the ancient teachers, and at the same time he has given that grammar a living speech. He has perceived in the Hebrew belief truths obscurely mirrored in Platonism. Yet the exclusiveness of Judaism bars the path of his progress. He has reached the wall of the universe in which he lives, and cannot overleap it. Beyond are the brethren to whom he would fain stretch out brotherly arms, but cannot. No farther could he go, nor could his successors, inferior to him, for he had journeyed straight to the limits within which they could only wander. But the path was made and the rampart attained which was to fall at the trumpet-sound of a victorious faith.

Alexandria, with her Greek and Hebrew philosophers,

early became a centre of Christian thought. Nowhere so much as here did the new religion grow and prosper. Nowhere did she receive so much from older modes of thought. The Platonist saw in Christianity a fuller and clearer embodiment of the noble Ideas of his philosophy than could be seen in Judaism ; the Hebrew saw in it the extension of the faith of Abraham and the promises to the whole race of man ; the Egyptian saw in it the great doctrines of the divine unity and man's future condition, which had only just disappeared from his religion in the shock of its contact with philosophy. The Greek vehicle which gave the expressions of Hebrew thought a definiteness they had hitherto wanted, yet which limited that luminous vagueness which has in it the living principle of development, was of necessity accepted by the Christianity as by the Judaism of Alexandria. But Hebrew thought reacted upon Greek form ; the first translations were the work of Hebrews, and the medium was deeply coloured by their use. Thus the Greek of the early Church was not purely Hellenic ; rather it was an intermediate mode of expression, retaining somewhat of the old expansiveness, marked by somewhat of the new limitation. Alexandrian speculation was not without a native influence. The Egyptian contributed his love of mystery, and that strong desire for individual holiness without reference to others which is the root of asceticism.

Two men are typical of this stirring age of the young Church in the Greek city. Clement of Alexandria, the learned Greek, eagerly read all philosophy, not to explain or to define dogma, but because he felt that the truth was to be discovered everywhere, in Greek and in Egyptian as well as in Hebrew writings. To him there was nothing derogatory to the Scriptures in the belief that there were other revelations, that indeed all wisdom was necessarily a gift of God. Had he reasoned out his view he would have been a modern of the moderns. As it is, he remains only a pious searcher, rejoicing in each fresh treasure that rewards his unwearying labour. In his simple nature and his true love of various knowledge combined, he stands quite alone among his fellows, to the loss of later generations, for had there been more like him, far less of ancient knowledge would have been allowed to perish.

Origen, like Clement, was a great and loving student, but he was more; he was one of the few original thinkers the world has known. He is of the school of Alexandria, yet one of ourselves, as the greatest men have no time or country, but are the true brethren of all mankind. He is of the Alexandrians, for by race an Egyptian, by training a Greek, by choice a Christian, he, the most learned man of the early Church, always remained Egyptian and Greek as well as Christian. He is one of us, and so the most interesting figure of his time, because he alone looked at the problems of theology with modern as well as with ancient eyes. He accepts the doctrines of Christianity, and uses philosophy for their definition ; so far he is ancient. Suddenly we see him calling on his reason and his moral sense to explain that which in its current form neither is willing to receive. Then he betakes himself to Hebrew criticism, and translates afresh every passage of Scripture bearing on his difficulty ; now he is modern. Thus it is with his famous argument in favour of the restitution of all things, which, be it remembered, he never advanced but as a theory, with modesty and reverence. But the argument, if it deal with that which is beyond man's reason, is well worth reading for its imaginative force and that finer tenderness which exalts him above his modern successors.

Origen was too learned and too deep a thinker for promotion. He held no place of honour or control; in his life he suffered from the suspicion of narrow minds; after his death, he was not added to the splendid roll of the saints; nor is it usual to consider the most profound philosopher, the most learned writer, the most laborious editor of the early Church, him whose wearied body held a soul of 'brazen' strength and 'adamantine' acuteness, as one of the Fathers, still less as one of the Doctors. Yet his fame shines out of ancient Alexandria like her far-seen Pharos, illuminating our way and warning us against its dangers.

These men lived in days when the state and the vulgar persecuted, but the philosophers sympathised. With the triumph of Christianity came the separation of the four schools of thought. The Hebrews, startled by the catastrophe of Jerusalem, had shrunk back into their old exclusiveness and so disappeared for centuries from the field of controversy. For the time their work was done. The philosophic and Egyptian parties united. Casting about for a religion for the vulgar, the philosophers were entrapped by the specious claims of the worship of Sarapis, and thus their works are now tinctured with superstition and magic to an extent which makes us wonder at the admiration with which many modern critics regard them. The Church having drawn from alien sources, no longer sought them as before. The influence of these sources was, however, felt long after they seemed to be dried up. Religion was strongly coloured by the definitions of philosophy, constantly increasing in precision, and by the introduction of asceticism. Hence arose the great controversies which raged in the early Church, and the new and false ideal of Christian life which we call monastic.

The first effect of the translation of the Old Testament was, as we have seen, to give so much of definite form to Hebrew thought as the Greek-speaking Hebrews were able to accept. The publication of the New Testament produced the same effect. But as the Christians studied philosophy and neglected Hebrew, this Greek tendency became more and more determinate. The very terms of theology were often philosophic, and had been the subjects of subtle analysis and keen discussion. Hence arose those debates which occupied the time and marred the usefulness of the Church for nearly five centuries, and which now we fail to understand. The questions which agitate believers of our day, such as the authority of the Church, the future condition of the dead, and a multitude of others, then never raised a doubt, except with some rare minds born before their time. Theologians busied themselves with deep mysteries now never discussed, then handled as though they had been matters capable of mathematical definition. As we think of these forgotten controversies, when their documents come before our eyes, we feel like a traveller who suddenly beholds a range of extinct volcanoes. The fires are quenched, and around their ashes rise the hollow walls which once glowed with ceaseless movement. There is no sign that they will ever be active again. Their life is gone, and they belong to the realm of the dead things of a forgotten age. In other regions other mountains are aglow, and enlighten while they threaten other fields and vineyards.

Yet more remarkable and more lasting was the return which the Egyptian religion made to Christianity when she offered the doubtful gift of asceticism. The system of a separate religious life in the seclusion of a convent is foreign to the instincts of the Shemites. Those among them who were bent on retirement always went from the peopled land to the silence of the desert. So did Elijah and the Baptist. Yet they returned in renewed strength to work among their fellow-men. There were then no hermits, still less were there convents. The sons of the prophets formed religious communities, and the Essenes had their separate villages; but neither of these were monastic establishments, they were rather associations of men, or men and women, who had a common purpose in life, or would live away from the distractions of the world.

In Egypt the fourth century suddenly shows us the hermit life and the conventual system in full vigour. It is significant that the first hermit, St. Antony, was an Egyptian, who did not speak Greek till he was past his twentieth year. It is much more significant that St. Pachomius, the founder of the first convent, was an Egyptian monk in an Egyptian convent before he embraced the new faith and carried into its practices the whole conventual system. That strange life, if life it may be called, shows in every aspect its double parentage, in its spiritual pride and its unworldliness, in its egotism and its generosity, in its indolence and its industry, its deadness and yet its vitality. It has never ceased to be

Egyptian, but it has never failed to be Christian. While we admit what we owe to its many virtues, the learned zeal which preserved the classics, and the missionary zeal which transformed the wild tribes of the Swiss valleys and the German forests, we must yet acknowledge the wretched indolence and selfish quietism which marked whole communities even in the most active times. Nor is it less remarkable to see how the two principles alternately triumphed, how a body of fierce inquisitors crossed the ocean, and became like Las Casas, the firm yet gentle protectors of the Indians against their Spanish oppressors.

Religion had been coloured by philosophy, dogma had been fixed, the monastic system had been instituted, the Hebrews had drawn away, and the philosophers were looking on in hostile apprehensiveness. Such was the state of Alexandrian opinion at the moment of the triumph of Christianity, when the scene of conflict was no longer without but within the Church. It was a time of great movements, in which we discern figures so large that distance cannot dwarf them, one indeed, the primate Athanasius, towering above the rest, the man of most personal influence throughout the Roman Empire between Julius Cæsar and Charlemagne. The heresy of Arius, a Libyan if not an Egyptian, was a compromise between Christianity and philosophy, which must have attracted the Hebrew and Greek elements in the Church, led by a man of intellectual acuteness and persuasive power. His opponent Athanasius, with inferior mental gifts, had a supreme skill in rousing the loyalty of his followers, an untiring energy, a tender tolerance, not rarely the gentle counterpoise of a fiery nature, and an entire forgetfulness of self. Throughout his most dramatic career he retained the simplicity of his youth. Persecuted and hunted down, five times an exile, and often in danger of his life, he triumphed at last, and died in peace, ruler of the patriarchal throne of Alexandria. He was neither Greek, nor Hebrew, nor Egyptian, but cast in the Roman mould; not a thinker or enthusiast or dreamer, but a man and a ruler of men.

The breach between the Church and the philosophers was now complete. It was made impassable by the ill fortune which gave the heathen party a temporary triumph under the auspices of the Emperor Julian, variously called the Apostate or the Philosopher. Julian was a man of politic compromises. He did not actively persecute the Church, but he set up the old religion of Sarapis under the protection of philosophy. All was overturned by his early death, except the mischief he had done. The Church had learnt nothing but to despise the philosophers, and at last began to persecute the harmless quietists, who still lingered about the precincts of the Museum. The defeated party wins our full sympathy when we witness the cruel death of Hypatia, beautiful, gentle, and learned, who may almost be called the last light of the Greek school of Alexandria. The mob had become the agent of the fanatical churchmen. The toleration of paganism had lately ceased with the sack of the temple of Sarapis; and now the teaching of philosophy was about to be proscribed.

The Church could not, however, destroy the philosophic tendency, which grew stronger and stronger within it. The theologians wrangled over insoluble points of doctrine, while learning was neglected and the state was in danger. When they had achieved the final separation of the Greek from the native Church, the Arabs came and the hostility of the Egyptians to their rulers made the conquest of Egypt easy. Alexandria alone offered a stout defence. When the city was taken and the Library burnt, her history ceases. Never afterwards the capital of Egypt, Alexandria only appears from time to time as a seat of commercial wealth. We read, indeed, how an Arab prince in the ninth century restored the Library and the University, as though the old institutions had risen from their ashes ; but in the vicissitudes of history there was no stability in this revival, and we hear of it no more.

Our own days witnessed a return of the greatness of Alexandria due to the establishment of the new route to India. The old city had shrunk to the space on the mole, when suddenly a new town grew on Alexander's mantle, an abode of Western merchants, not beautiful, but with the stateliness of wealth in the great square and the long lines of broad streets. The later Pelusium, Port Saïd, on the ample harbour of the canal of the two seas, despite a better site, fever-stricken by the air of Lake Menzeleh, could not rival the older city. Then came, as in the Roman time, revolt and the interference of the West, Alexandria once more the centre of resistance, once more stricken the hardest blow, and in the destruction of the new town, the latest proof of the wanton temper of the Alexandrian mob.

Unlike Rome and Athens, Alexandria has scarcely a

trace of her ancient magnificence. Had her edifices been Egyptian, they would not have disappeared, but at the capital the Greek kings and the Roman emperors built as Greeks, and not as Egyptians. Thus while their temples stand in Upper Egypt in massive splendour, the capital is almost without record of their rule. Fragments or sites alone recall her splendid edifices. At the entrance of the Great Harbour a lighthouse still marks the place of the famous Pharos of Alexandria. Of the Museum and Library, the Palaces, the royal mausoleum, and the Temple of Sarapis, there are no remains which can be recognised, unless indeed the recent discovery of a great sepulchral vault has brought to light part of the royal burial-place. Of the obelisks removed from older cities to adorn the new capital, a pair remained till our own time, one standing, the other fallen. Modern taste has despoiled Alexandria of these striking monuments, to set them up apart in London and in New York, amid uncongenial surroundings. The great column which is commonly known as Pompey's Pillar yet stands, raised by the prefect of Egypt in honour of Diocletian, probably when he recovered the country after the revolt of the usurper or patriot Achilleus. It is nearly a hundred feet high, the shaft being a single block of red granite. In the environs may be seen the remains of an interesting monument, the temple of Queen Arsinoë as Aphrodite on the promontory of Zephyrium, near Ramleh, 'the Sandy,' a favourite resort of the Alexandrian merchants of our day. The position is very striking, on a high cliff looking over the sea towards Cyprus, the island of the goddess here worshipped. In the quiet of the ruin, where the silence of the desert coast is only broken by the murmur of the waves on the sandy shore below, memory recalls the tale which gives this temple a place in history. When Euergetes went away on his great expedition into the far east, Queen Berenice here vowed if her husband returned in safety, to dedicate her beautiful hair to the sea-born goddess to whom the sailors prayed. The vow was kept, and the long golden tresses hung up within the temple. Some daring thief, who feared neither goddess nor king, carried off the costly offering. Ptolemy, enraged by the loss, sought in vain, until Conon, the state astronomer, discovered Berenice's hair, not at Alexandria, but in the sky, as a string of stars. The stars had been there of old, and were only separated as a new constellation by depriving the Lion of his tail;

yet the conceit satisfied the king; and astronomy has retained this curious memorial of the faithful pair.

At Alexandria, after the custom of travellers, we say farewell to Egypt. At every other ancient site we have learnt something of the marvellous history of the country, in itself most interesting, and touching in turn the history of every great nation of the old world. Here at Alexandria all is summed up, and Egypt passes away from our sight where she completed her work and gave her manifold knowledge to the world, more definite through the skill of the scholars of the Museum, more human through the faith of the fathers of the Church. While other sites are Egyptian, Alexandria is in turn Greek and Hebrew also, but most of all Christian, of the family which knows no nationality but that of our universal humanity. Nowhere are we more sensible of the dignity of ancient history, which takes us away from the trifling events of our time and country to see within a broader horizon the larger movements of nations as they work out the Divine decrees.

CHRONOLOGICAL SKETCH.

THE chronology of ancient Egypt is as yet undetermined, the best authorities differing by many centuries as to the whole duration of the monarchy. The basis of reckoning is still the list of Thirty Dynasties under which the native historian Manetho arranged the kings. A comparison with the evidence of the monuments and papyri has shown that this list was drawn up from good sources, but is, in its present condition, hopelessly corrupt. All that we can as yet do is to group the Dynasties under great periods, of more or less uncertain duration, until we reach the age of the Empire, the reckonings of the rise of which do not greatly differ. From that time the dates are more and more exact, though but one of the Thirty Dynasties, the Twenty-seventh, can be absolutely fixed in its beginning to a particular year.

It is usual to arrange the Dynasties in a tabular form. This is objectionable, as we do not know whether some of them did not overlap others, while it is probable that a few were wholly contemporary with one another. A statement is therefore here given in preference to a table, as admitting of more clear explanation. The designation of Dynasties as Thinite, Memphite, Theban, &c. is avoided, because it tends to confuse the city of the origin of a family with the chief city or true capital.

I.
PRE-MONUMENTAL AGE.

(Dynasties I., II., and greater part of III.)—Duration, 800 or 700 years (?). Capital of Egypt, Memphis.

II.
MEMPHITE KINGDOM.

Under Pyramid-builders (latter part of Dyn. III., IV., V., VI.)—700 or 600 yrs. Memphis.

III.
OBSCURE PERIOD.

(Dyn*. VII., VIII., IX., X.)—Capital at first Memphis (VII., VIII.); then Hanes or Heracleopolis (IX., X.) According to Manetho, Dyns. IX. and X. were of Heracleopolite kings, and the absence of monuments at Memphis implies the decay of that city and the transfer of the capital. This age is wholly without remains. We do not know if the Dynasties were contemporary (VII. and VIII. with IX. and X.) or successive, and the length of time they filled is unknown.

IV.

THEBAN KINGDOM.

(Dyn*. XI., XII., XIII.)—Capital, Thebes; at first provincial, afterwards of the whole country. The rise (XI.), the greatness (XII.), and the decline (XIII.) of the Thebans is marked by the division into Dynasties. The middle period (XII.) is certain (213 yrs.), the others unknown. It is possible that the XIVth Dynasty of Xoïtes succeeded the Thebans and preceded the Shepherds.

V.

SHEPHERD-RULE.

(Dyn*. XV., XVI., contemporary with XVII., Theban, and perhaps with XIV., Xoïtes).—Capital, Zoan or Tanis. Length of Shepherd-rule probably 511 years; at the close Egypt divided between (XVI.) Shepherds and (XVII.) Thebans.

VI.

THE EMPIRE.

(Dyn*. XVIII., XIX., XX., in part.)—Capital, Thebes. B.C. cir. 1600 to 1150.

VII.

THE DECLINE.

(Dyn. XX., part, to XXX.)—B.C. cir. 1150 to cir. 345
The chief dates are the following :—

Sheshonk I., or Shishak (XXII.), rise of Bubastites	B.C. cir. 970
Ethiopian conquest of Pianchi	,, ,, 750
Psammetichus I., rise of Saïtes (XXVI.)	,, ,, 665
Conquest by Cambyses (XXVII.)	,, ,, 527
Independence (XXVIII.–XXX.)	,, ,, 404 ?
Conquest by Ochus	,, ,, 345 ?

NOTES.

Page 129. From the expressions in the 'Dictionnaire Géographique,' especially p. 919, one would be disposed to put Dr. Brugsch's modification in a definite form; but since the publication in 1878 of the part of the work referred to, the second English edition of the 'History of Egypt' (1881) puts the case less positively (ii. p. 421 seqq.). As the author well remarks, survey and excavation are needed to settle the geography of the route of the Exodus (p. 432).

Page 134. I am aware that Dr. Brugsch considers the sacred name of On to be Pe-Tum, the Abode of Tum, and places Pe-Ra, the Abode of Ra, to the northward. ('Dict. Géogr.' under reff. On, Heliopolis.) The difficulties of this view, which separates On from Heliopolis, make me rather hold that the two names designate two temples and quarters of Heliopolis.

Page 147. Dr. Brugsch, agreeing with the lamented Mariette, maintains the primitive cultivation of the balsam-trees near Heliopolis, on the strength of an early hieroglyphic inscription. ('Dict. Géogr.' p. 1279.) If so, there was probably a continuous cultivation till the Arab times, and the relations of Herod with Cleopatra would naturally have led to the employment of Hebrew gardeners for their famous native trees.

Page 202. The important discovery that St. Pachomius was originally an Egyptian heathen recluse is due to M. Revillout ('Rev. Ég.' i. p. 160). The 'Revue Égyptologique' is full of information of the highest value, derived from Coptic and Demotic as well as Hieroglyphic sources.

www.ingramcontent.com/pod-product-compliance
Lightning Source LLC
Chambersburg PA
CBHW042127160426
43198CB00021B/2936